A

to Your Bowling Score

Add 30 Pins
to Your Bowling Score

by

Billy Welu
with Jerry Levine

Fully Illustrated

CROWN PUBLISHERS, INC.

New York

Printed in the United States of America

ISBN: 0-517-504758

Library of Congress Catalog Card Number: 73-168302

Published simultaneously in Canada
by General Publishing Company Limited

All line drawings by Chris Simon

10   9   8

Contents

Preface

Bowling has been a popular pastime since the days when Babylonians set things afire and Egyptian kings were laying plans to be laid to rest. Most bowling books with an instructional theme start with historical references and move from there into vague tutoring and bland statements. You'll find no historical undertones in the pages that follow. You will find only what I hope will be the most revealing, all-encompassing work on bowling ever produced.

When you have finished reading the book—please don't run right through it as if it were a novel—there is no doubt you will be a better bowler. For too many years too many bowlers have contented themselves with going through the motions without really knowing what the game is all about. You'll be amazed at some of the things you will learn and you'll soon be aware that an application of what you have learned will show up on the lanes.

With the proper amount of training—make that "regimentation"—and with a comprehension of what you are doing, your game will show an immediate and startling improvement. Meaning, of course: your average will show an upturn. A *sharp* upturn, if you will. And that's what the game is all about— proving yourself out on the lanes.

There is no sport that comes close to bowling in its appeal to so many people and so many kinds of people. Occasional polls taken by those grinding axes for other participant sports always pinpoint the ancient game of kegling as the one that appeals to more people than any other. If you are statistics-minded, a nice round figure of those that go bowling on a regular basis is forty million.

It's only right that you ask the reason for its great popularity. Why is it that there aren't more golfers? Or surfers? Or sky divers? What are the qualities of bowling that make it reach out and touch so many people?

Not many games other than bowling and billiards place absolutely no restrictions on its practitioners. None whatsoever. You can start out when you are eight and keep going until you are eighty. The game requires no strength, and its price structure precludes no one. A woman bowler can get to be almost as good as a male bowler and there are built-in ego-swellers that bring out the hero urge within all of us.

Medical men say the therapeutic and physical values bowling offers are unrivaled. It's a moderate form of exercise that stimulates mind and body to the degrees you require stimulation. You may play the game any time of the day, any day of the week, any time of the year. And when it rains or snows, you won't be troubled until you leave the bowling center and race for your car.

There are bowlers whose averages belie their physiques and determination, and there are bowlers who score quite well even though they're overweight and seem quite lackadaisical. That's another unique feature of the sport: champions don't always look like champions. There are variations to the game that have never before been brought to the attention of the book-buying public. Until now, that is.

Bowlers come in assorted talents; they are also categorized as novice, intermediate, or professional. The aim here—in text, photos, and diagrams—is to bring all categories closer together, at least as far as knowledge of bowling is concerned. The beginner will learn how to overcome those things he has been doing wrong, so that he may be able to rise to the next level of proficiency. The intermediate will be apprised as to how he can take his game from the midaverage range and advance to a level that could enable him to attain professional status.

And for the bowler who feels he has reached his peak, there will be something, too. There are elements to—and in—bowling that, perhaps, even he is unaware of: the way the game has changed, the conditioning of lanes, how to adjust, ball weighting, and much else. This is the first time all the loose ends of bowling have been tied together in one book; the result will be higher spirits—and higher averages—for everyone.

1.

The Game of Bowling

THE people who operate bowling centers go to great lengths to get people to come in and try the game. They know that once they get the neophyte to toss that first ball, they have probably captured him for life. What the proprietor does, then, is to make available the equipment the bowler will need to play the game and to get thorough enjoyment out of what he or she is doing. There probably is no parallel in any other sport, for the proprietor—your host for the day—offers the equipment for a comparatively nominal charge.

Exactly what are you going to need when you start bowling? Let's assume that you have graduated from those first few outings when you've borrowed one of the bowling balls provided free of charge, or rented for a nominal fee a pair of bowling shoes. That's right. That's all you need. A ball, the proper kind of shoes, and a bag to carry them in, and you're on your way. Let's get right into just what you need, should use, and should wear.

Equipment

There was a time when the bowler had absolutely no choice when it came to choosing a ball. You went in and purchased black or you purchased nothing at all. All that has changed now and it certainly has been a change for the better. While in the main the male bowler still chooses the conventional black ball, many now go in for balls with hues and tones. As for the kids and ladies, however, there is an unbelievable variety.

Bowling balls today are speckled and mottled and seeded with rich colors. Their consistency, though, is another story and here's where you have to decide which ball will do more for you (knock down more pins) after you've decided which ball looks better to you.

Bowling balls are made of either rubber or plastic. There always is a hard core of rubber at the center of a ball and then layers of cork and rubber are intermingled. Plastic balls are made from a mold. All bowling-ball manufacturers turn out balls in both plastic and rubber, and when they created two different kinds their reasoning was twofold. Initially, they were catering to the distaff bowler who sought to escape from the ordinary by tossing a ball that often was color coordinated with her bowling attire.

Then, too, there was another thought in mind. With so many more people coming into the game, and with almost everyone using a black ball, time that could have best been used in bowling was lost as bowlers fumbled and turned and hefted balls to see which one was theirs. But it is easy for a bowler to pick out his ball when his is green and his teammates have blue, black, red, or even see-through plastic balls.

But once a steady flow of plastic balls began—and keep in mind that almost always it's the plastic ball that comes in bright colors—it began to have a telling effect on scoring. When the lane was dry, the plastic hooked much more than the rubber ball.

Before that gets too complicated, a word of advice. When you get around to buying your first bowling ball, choose one with a color that suits you. Many a new bowler has blamed his poor bowling on a ball that just wasn't the right color. You and I know there's no credibility to this, but if it affects his or her game then it's just the wrong ball. Mood, temperament, and emotion play too strong a role in bowling to treat color lightly.

Once you've reached a degree of proficiency that indicates that you might want to go further, by all means get yourself a rubber ball. For maximum hitting power, consistency of roll, and the properties that will enable you to adjust to ever-changing lane conditions, plastic cannot measure up to rubber. At least, that's the way I feel.

Naturally, bowling balls come in assorted weights. Just as a baseball player has to decide which weight bat is best for him and the golfer the correct weight to his club, so must the bowler choose his ball. The bowling-ball manufacturers do yeoman service in this department, offering their black or multi-hued balls in weights that range from eight to sixteen pounds. It goes without saying that the youngster who first tries to bowl cannot be expected to lift a ball much heavier than eight pounds. (There is no variance, of course, to the circumference; that's a rigid specification.)

As the bowler's expertise increases and as he gets older and stronger, he will want to move on to a heavier ball. There's no denying that the heavier the ball the more pins will be knocked down. Bear in mind this additional fact: not all of the better bowlers toss a sixteen-pound ball. When lane conditions vary, and a bowler feels he is getting too much or too little on the ball in the release, he may well start using a ball that weighs a bit less. Some of the top professionals use a ball that varies between fifteen and sixteen pounds.

Okay. You've selected the ball in the color and weight that is best suited to you. What next? Well, you must have the proper kind of shoes. Here, too, the manufacturers have come to the aid of a fashion-conscious bowling public. Shoes come in a variety of styles and colors, all in keeping with the theme that bowlers want to look attractive as well as bowl well. With the very essence of good bowling being a smooth slide on your last step, it's only logical that all bowling shoes have leather soles on the corresponding sliding foot. If you are a right-handed bowler, the shoe you purchase—or rent—will enable you to slide on the left foot. Sliding too much, or not enough, or not at all should there be a foreign substance on the approach can be ruinous to your game and there are numerous instances in which a bowler has hurt himself.

Bowling-shoe manufacturers go to great lengths to put quality into their product. There are firms that market devices that slip onto the shoe to promote smooth sliding; bowlers who have attained a high degree of perfection in their game go still further. Should the bowler fear too long a slide, he may have the heel on his sliding foot built up to inhibit this action. Or, should the reverse be true—not enough slide—he may have the height of the heel reduced to give him more free-wheeling action. The rubber heel serves as a brake.

Here's something many of the better bowlers don't know. You can even have a sole made of a soft felt applied to your shoe to make for a truer slide. Quite a few of the bowlers on the Professional Bowlers Association circuit have done just that and it has never failed to help their game, if only for psychological reasons. Bowling can be as simple or as sophisticated as you choose to make it.

One further note on shoes: with Teflon and similar products having made such an impact on the American scene, it was only natural that this nonstick substance should find its way into bowling. At least one company turns out a Teflon sole that is made to adhere to the sliding shoe. If you have a fixation about getting a proper slide, it's something you may want to look into.

At the outset, though. find a shoe that is comfortable, looks good on you, and will take the wear and tear of being put on, taken off, packed away, and often keeping company in the same bag with a sixteen-pound bowling ball.

Let's move on now to another aspect of the bowling scene— the proper attire—how to dress, what to wear to be able to bowl your best. Don't make light of this. The right or wrong clothes can have a beneficial or devastating effect on your game. In one case, the wrong slacks conceivably cost a professional bowler a championship in the finals of a televised tournament.

The bowler—a well-known young fellow—was competing in the last game of a tournament that had been in progress for four days. It was midway in the final match and there were many thousands of dollars at stake, as well as the publicity that goes with capturing a big tournament viewed by millions of people. As the bowler let go on his first shot, the inseam of his slacks tore right down to the knee. Naturally, there was no time to permit him to change pants or to have them sewn. He was forced to finish out the game that way.

Being a shy person, the pro never seemed to be the same for the rest of the game. He was so self-conscious he was unable to get back the expertise that had marked his play throughout the entire event. He lost the game and the championship and everything else that went with it.

Of course, that may be a rare incident, but it points up the need to be attired properly when bowling. A loose-fitting shirt is ideal—one that doesn't in any way restrict the arm swing.

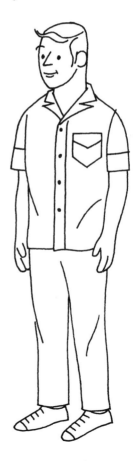

Loose-fitting shirt and slacks are essential when bowling. There's too much stooping and bending and stretching involved for the bowler to be restricted by tight clothing

When it comes time to order your league shirt, don't allow vanity to dictate size. If you make a mistake, it should be toward a larger size. Here, too, the manufacturers come to the rescue of the bowler; they will almost always build a few extra inches into the critical places on a bowling shirt. But you should verify this. In all instances, only a short-sleeved shirt will do.

As for slacks, remember the case of the professional who lost the title. Wear only comfortable slacks and be certain that they're not made of a stiff material. All too often the synthetics look fine but prove restrictive. The ideal slacks are knits, and when there is enough of a selection in your size and color, try to get a double knit. They feel great, look great, and they give in all the right places when you bend down and let the ball fly toward the pins.

Where to Bowl

Okay. You've got your ball, and your shoes, and you're dressed perfectly. Now what? Easy. Walk or drive to the nearest bowling center. Or to the one where all your friends go. Just so you won't be completely unaware of the size and shape of things, here are a few vital statistics about the lanes you'll find in any establishment you visit.

First, they cost many thousands of dollars to construct. And that includes those amazing machines at the other end—the ones that do all the work a pinboy used to do, but better and faster and more efficiently. The approach—the area where you take your stance, go into your footwork, and then release the ball—is usually sixteen feet in length. This is more than enough room for any bowler, big or small. From the foul line to the first pin is sixty feet. If you want to relate the distance to some other sport, this is about the same distance a pitcher fires the ball to home plate.

The approach and the lane itself is constructed of a series of boards layed side by side. There is no special name for them; they're called boards by everyone, but they're vital to the bowler's performance. Later you'll learn how to use the boards to knock down pins. Today there are thirty-nine boards to every lane. They are one inch wide, and like everything else you see, they're made of wood. At some older places, you may still find forty, even forty-one boards. In some alleys the lane itself was an inch or two wider, and in others perhaps the boards were slightly less than one inch wide. For our purposes, we will deal only with thirty-nine boards.

Naturally, these dimensions do not include the gutter, or channel, as it is commonly called these days. But you're all going to be so proficient at bowling that the channels will never be a factor!

The center at which you bowl is a monument to efficiency. The activity of hundreds of people is maintained in an orderly fashion, sometimes for twenty-four hours every day, seven days a week. All have restaurants and most have cocktail lounges; all the needs of bowlers are served. With few exceptions there is even a nursery where mom can leave her young

From the foul line to the headpin is sixty feet

one under the supervision of a nurse or matron. When it comes to bowling itself, all centers offer instruction. Many places have a pro shop on the premises where equipment may be purchased and where friendly, professional counsel is offered.

The bowling proprietor is in the service business and it's always good business to provide the finest of service. The proprietor is a host, the father image to some kids, an organizer and a bon vivant. Give him a chance and he'll be your good time custodian. Bowling always has been good, clean, and inexpensive fun.

Whom to Bowl With

There are two distinct ways in which you may pursue the game. One is called open bowling, the other league competition. Which you choose depends only on how you can regiment your time. Open bowling means that any time you and your pals feel like it, you just trot off to the lanes and bowl. It's as simple as that. It can be as competitive as you make it. League bowling is another matter.

This means that you and others like you have banded together to roll under supervision, at a specific time, on a specified day of the week. No variations are permitted here. If your league bowls Tuesday nights, starting at 6:30, that's the very latest you can get there. And you'll be doing it for about two-thirds of the year, for league seasons usually run from September through May—though there are also summer leagues of much shorter duration.

There is absolutely no reason why the novice should not join a league. All you have to do is hook up with other bowlers like yourself . . . with a minimal amount of experience or, if you are experienced, with an advanced group. Bowlers always help newcomers, and just by competing with a team in a league where the accent is on teamwork and accomplishment you'll find your game will pick up almost immediately.

A great way to launch yourself into bowling is to go directly to an instructor. A terribly wrong thing to do would be to go bowling with a bunch of friends who haven't learned the techniques of the game. Once you learn bad habits, you'll have a difficult time breaking them. It's easier not to start than to stop nail-biting.

An instructor will personalize his tutoring. He'll suggest variations and nuances depending on your physique, the length of your arm, your height and weight, and so on. It will be comforting for you to know that if and when problems begin to develop in your game—and it happens to everyone, even the pros —you can go right back to that very same instructor and have him work with you to correct the errors. He may even recommend that you join a league immediately, so as not to lose out on the fun generated by league activity.

It goes without saying that the 200 game you shoot or the final-frame strike you chalk up will have much more significance to you and others when it has helped your team win a game and perhaps keep you in first place or get you close to the top of the standings. How long will it take before you roll your first 300 game? I'm afraid that the overwhelming odds only diminish when one becomes a professional.

The standard bowling team is comprised of five persons. There are never more on a team, but you can descend from there to four- and three-man competition and on down into doubles play and even a singles league. Which you join depends on what kind of leagues they're forming where and when you want to bowl. Another factor to consider is that the more people you roll with, the longer the league session will last. Usually you will shoot three games, but four and five and six are often the rule in play where there are only two and three to a team.

Practically all leagues have a prize fund to which you contribute in addition to the price of bowling. The money collected can go for trophies and cash awards at season's end. Some leagues have a banquet following the last session and others put money into a vacation fund that can later be used by players to go to some far-off place to relax and rehash the bowling year just ended.

Here's something to consider when you decide which kind of

league you want to roll in: your average probably will be a bit higher in a doubles or singles league. The reason for this is that sometimes in five-man competition it's hard to maintain your concentration throughout a whole session. Stray thoughts creep into your mind and you may not be keyed in at all times. In doubles and singles play you can get into a groove and stay there longer, for there just isn't as much time between shots to divert your concentration. On the other hand, when you do something noteworthy, you'll receive many more accolades and pats on the back if you have four teammates.

Another form of league play is the mixed league where boys and girls, men and women compete together. The stress in these leagues is on fun as well as scoring. In almost all instances a bowler's score will dip—sometimes sharply—in mixed league play. You'll have to decide if a diminution in your average is worth the fun and frivolity. To a man—and woman—bowlers agree that the real purpose in bowling is to provide fun, and if a mixed league offers you more, then by all means join one.

Scoring

This may sound incredible, but there are people who have tried their hand at bowling and then given it up because, they stated, it was too difficult to keep score. Don't you believe it. Scoring is almost as simple as the mechanics of the game, which is to hit something with something. If you start out with one simple rule, you'll never again have any trouble keeping score.

A spare is worth 10 points, plus the amount of pins knocked down on the very next ball. A strike is worth 10 points plus the amount of pins knocked down on the next *two* balls. That's all there is. It's that elementary. You have only to remember that when a spare is thrown you have to mark a score down right after the next ball. After a strike you do nothing until *two* more balls have been tossed.

The ultimate achievement in bowling is a 300 game; let's see how this scoring would proceed.

Naturally, you'd have thrown a strike on your very first ball, for in order to have a perfect game you'd have to throw twelve strikes in succession. After your first-frame strike, you wait until two more shots have been taken. The next shot, of course, is a strike. You do nothing. The next shot (the second after that opening strike) is a strike. So, you score 10 for the first strike, plus 10 more for each of the next two shots, or a total of 30 in the first box (frame). Now you have a strike in the second frame, but the bowler has tossed only *one* more ball since then so you have to wait until the next shot. It's a strike, naturally, so he gets 10 for the second-frame strike, plus 20 more pins for strikes in the third and fourth frames, for another 30 and a total of 60 in the second frame. And that's the way it keeps going right up to and through the tenth frame. A strike in the tenth box earns two more attempts. Put all those 30s together and you have a 300, perfection in bowling.

As for the spare, you get instant results. Get a spare in the opening frame and 9 on your next shot and you earn 10 and 9 for 19. Get a spare in the first frame (or any frame, of course) and follow it with a strike and you earn 20 pins for the frame in which you spared. Then, of course, you will wait two more shots before marking down a tally in the frame in which you've recorded a strike. A last-frame spare earns, like all its predecessors, one more shot.

As for most other games, there are traditions and superstitions bowlers follow; this makes bowling more fun. One of these is never to mark down those 30s in any one frame when a bowler is on a string (a succession of strikes). You just wait until he has failed to get a strike and then you start filling in his scores.

Part of the fun of scoring—and also an integral part of the game—is learning all the symbols. They tell a story about how each game went. You should learn all of them; learn to use them, learn to read them. They could indicate to you when you get careless during any given game, when you miss easy spares, and how good—or bad—you are at making difficult shots.

Taking those symbols one by one, they are:

Spare	Strike	Split	Converted split	Error
◺	⊠	◯	⦸	—

The spare and strike we've already delved into. Let's discuss what the others mean and when you should mark them down in the little boxes in the upper righthand portion of each frame.

A split means that after you've thrown your first ball, the headpin is down and one or more pins are down between the two or more pins that remain upright. A variation is if at least one pin is down immediately ahead of two or more pins still standing. If you make or convert the split, you simply divide the circle with the slash that indicates spare. It's sort of a feather in your cap when your score shows one or more of those symbols.

That leaves only the error and if you never—or hardly ever —have these appear in your score, you're on your way toward being a much better bowler. Or you've already arrived. Pros and higher averaged bowlers predicate their game on stringing those strikes, but they also know that not every ball tossed can be a strike ball and they've got to ring up those spares to keep their scores at a healthy level.

Let's wrap up this lesson on scoring with a game that incorporates all five symbols we've set down. When you've read this portion, take a few minutes out and make up your own game. Through repetition you'll have absolutely no trouble in applying what you've absorbed to a real game.

For openers, you've knocked down eight pins on your first ball. Second shot in the first frame you knock down the two remaining pins. Give yourself a spare; you're on your way.

Second frame: Nine on the first ball. Give yourself 19 in the first frame. Second shot: you miss the one pin standing. Shame on you. Give yourself an error and 28 in the second frame.

Third frame: A strike. Good going. Give yourself an X in that little box.

Fourth frame: Another strike. Great. But don't do anything yet in that third frame; you still have one more shot coming.

Fifth frame: Nine on the first ball. Not too bad. Take 10 pins for each of your strikes (third and fourth frames), add the 9 to that for 29 and add it to the 28 you've marked down for 57 in the third frame. On your second shot in this frame you get the spare, so that means in the fourth frame you get 10 for the strike, 10 for the spare and you now add 20 to the 57 for 77.

Sixth frame: You topple 8 pins, leaving a split. Take 10 for the spare, plus 8, and add the 18 to the 77 for 95 in the fifth. On the second shot in the frame you make that tough split and you have a spare going for you once again.

Seventh frame: Another strike. Give yourself 10 for the strike, 10 for the previous spare and add 20 to the 95 for 115 in the sixth.

Eighth frame: Another strike. Do nothing. You still have one more shot coming on your seventh frame strike.

Ninth frame: One more strike. That's three in a row, so you get 30 pins added to what you had in the sixth, giving you 145 in the seventh.

Tenth frame: First ball you knock down 7 pins. You get 10 for each strike in the eighth and ninth frames, plus the 7 pins on the first shot in the tenth. That's 27 added to the 145, giving you 172 in the eighth. Second shot in the tenth frame, you pick up the spare, so give yourself 20 more pins in the ninth, 10 for the strike, 10 for the spare. Now you have 192 in the ninth and one more shot coming because of that spare in the tenth. Last ball—another strike, giving you 20 more pins in the final frame for a grand total of 212.

Now, here's the way that imaginary game we've just described will look:

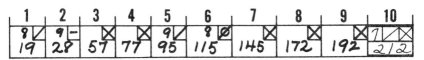

One more time and let's see if you have it. A strike gives you 10 pins, plus the amount of pins you knock down on the next two balls. A spare gives you 10 pins plus what you knock down on the very next shot. That's all there is to it.

Safety and Courtesy

It doesn't matter what kind of bowler you are, where you bowl, or the kind of league in which you participate. There are hard-and-fast rules in every sport, and these exist in bowling, too. In fact, adhering strictly to the rules and regulations probably is more important in bowling. It's a game of extreme concentration and even though you are alone on the approach and it's you against the pins, at the same time there may be as many as 30, 40, or 50 bowlers on either side of you whose actions and scoring are interdependent on how you conduct yourself.

Horseplay on the lanes is taboo. Don't ever believe that horseplay goes hand in hand with having fun. Don't be raucous; a pat on the back and a friendly word are always in vogue. Don't be a sore loser and a poor winner. The best bowler is the one who recognizes achievement in others, accepts defeat gracefully, and knows at all times how to distinguish between the two.

For the most part, good bowling procedure is dictated by common sense. You will know instinctively what is expected of you and what you should not be doing. Let's touch on a few of the items covering safety and courtesy.

Whenever you are bowling, whether in open or league action, the bowler on the right always has preference. That is not to say that if you get up first and are lining up your shot that you have to step back and off the approach if the man on the right steps up for his shot. Once you are there, you bowl. However, if there is any question as to who got there first, it's always the man on the right who has the right of way.

There is one variation to that rule, but that will come into play only should you graduate to the ranks of the Professional Bowlers Association. Because there is such intense concentration on every shot, a bowler competing in a professional tournament would defer to one pair of lanes on either side. That means that where courtesy in open and normal league play is extended to the man on the right, in the pro ranks the man to the left receives the same privilege.

There was a time when all the bowling books and all the old-timers cautioned—make that warned—everyone about chewing gum while sitting in the settee area. Mustn't chew gum, they said; it may fall out of your mouth or miss the trash receptacle, or what have you. That was about as realistic as telling a bowler he shouldn't use that greasy kid stuff on his hair, for it might drip on the approach.

By all means chew gum if it helps relieve the tensions that will build up while you are bowling. And tobacco, if you like it and it helps. And snuff, or anything that will fight pressure and fatten your score. Here again, let your common sense and normal behavior govern what you do. Obviously, you wouldn't want to spill your glass of soda or cup of coffee on the approach, and certainly you would not want to mar the surface with your chewing gum.

Any foreign substance that reaches the bowling area could be extremely hazardous should a bowler pull up short because his shoe has picked it up. Do your eating and drinking behind the settee area and you and your teammates—and your opponents—will be safe from harm. Beat the other guy out on the lanes, not in the settee area.

Though it might seem like a simple procedure, don't minimize the importance of how to pick up the ball from the rack, or turntable. Even the best and most experienced bowlers are often derelict in this and it could result in serious, perhaps permanent injury.

Picking up the ball. Always use both hands, with palms held at right angles to the ball return

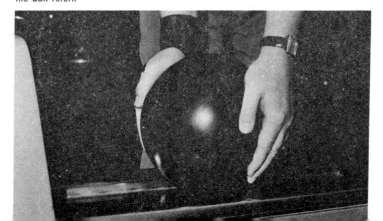

The ball you'll be tossing at least twelve times a game (if you're lucky and get all strikes) weighs up to sixteen pounds. That's quite a bit of weight and, if you'll permit a play on words, it should not be taken lightly. When you lift the ball from the rack preparatory to bowling, never put your hands—that's right, *hands,* not one hand—on the ball so that they could be struck by a ball returning from the other end of the lane. Always make your approach from the side and lift the ball so that even an onrushing ball cannot catch your fingers. This is another exercise in common sense.

In the final analysis, the way you would comport yourself in everyday circumstances will be more than sufficient to see you through any normal bowling session. There will be offshoots to what we have said and there will be crises arising. When they do, see if you can't come up with the proper solution. If you can't, ask an experienced bowler—though even the pros constantly are being called on to improvise.

On several occasions there was some sticky matter on the approaches. Usually, the host bowling center has on hand a supply of steel wool with which the substance may be scraped off. There was a time when none was available, however, and it remained for one enterprising pro bowler to solve the problem. He dipped his hand in the ash tray and applied ashes to the sole of the shoe on his sliding foot. This did the trick, enabled him to slide properly. The innovation has since spread and many a time you'll see a better bowler ensure his slide by applying cigarette ash to his shoe.

Pros combat the reverse problem—too much slide—in a unique manner. They'll rough up the sole with a sharp implement and often cut grooves into the heel so that they'll be able to stop more quickly.

Most pros have no problem at the foul line these days, making sure they come to a full stop six or eight inches behind it. A few years back I pulled up short on a sticky approach and wrenched my back; it put me out of commission for a few tournaments. It might serve you well to check your shoe and approach *each time* you get set to deliver a ball. The pros do.

2.

Improving Your Game

NOW that we've discussed the basics of bowling—the things all of us had to learn before plunging into the sport—it's time to move on to the next level. The refinements you will learn, the secrets you will be privileged to hear in some instances will amaze you. Except for the sport's hierarchy, some of the topics to be touched on have never before been put into print.

Success in any venture cannot be achieved without diligence and patience. This rule holds true for bowling as well as for any other sport. Every emotion is brought into play, concentration is an extremely vital factor, and skill in a multitude of aspects of the game is hard to learn.

The following chapters and sections are for every bowler—novice, intermediate, and professional. Even if you've seen or heard some of the detailed information before, now you will have it all in one book to use as a reference, to enable you finally to raise your average to an impressive level, and to make you as well versed in the sport as you always wanted to be.

Stance and Steps

Before you do anything else, you must learn how far back from the foul line you should line up and take your stance before going into your approach and delivery. Let's call it "the point of origin," for that's exactly what it is. Leave your ball on the rack and walk up to the foul line. Place the heels of both feet a few inches from the line and then take four normal steps

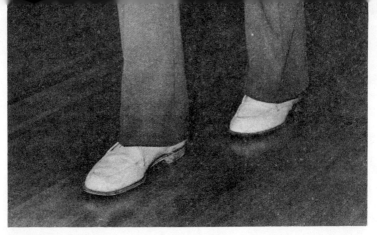

The first step—make it short

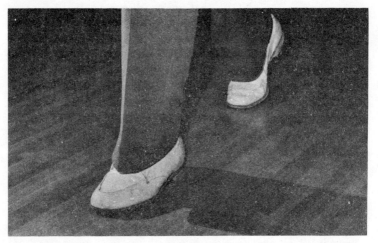

The second step—a little longer, but not too fast

back toward the approach area. Don't exaggerate the length of the steps; don't make them too long; don't take mincing steps. Four normal strides. Then, when you've done that, toss in an extra half step. That'll take care of the slide, which really is the most critical stage of the four-step delivery.

The four-step delivery is recommended for everyone, for it will best allow you to coordinate with your arm swing. These two motions are the core of your bowling; I can't stress too strongly devoting much time to them. The arm swing itself breaks down into four segments, so it is only logical that each movement be integrated with one step.

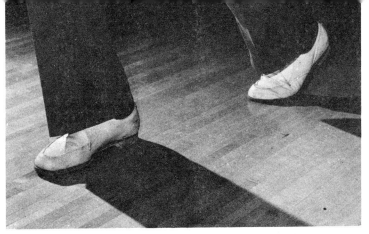

The third step—all set to go, make this one a bit faster than the first two

The fourth step—arm and ball should arrive at the same time

A different view of the fourth step

Timing is of so crucial a nature that the four parts of the arm swing should be labeled. They are the push-away, down-swing, backswing, and follow-through.

You should not necessarily alter your game to conform to this four-step pattern. Some of our finest bowlers use a three-, or five-, or even six-step delivery. One of the finest bowlers around some years ago—a fellow named Stan Gifford—went everyone a few better; he had a shuffling style that amounted to some ten steps. If your game is already sound and you don't use four steps, don't. If you want to know why four steps are better, let's go on.

Naturally, some bowlers will be farther from the foul line after their four and one half steps then others. Taller fellows will take longer steps, shorter ones shorter steps. Remember this point, though, about your first step: Make that opening movement quite short. It's sole purpose is to break your inertia and get you into motion. It's like the first step on the dance floor as you pick up the beat of the band. Think of it as getting you into the rhythm and remember that it's *your* rhythm, the one you will continue to follow for as many years as you go bowling.

The Arm Swing

On that first step you have to get that ball moving. The trick here—we call it trick, for all too many people fear they need Herculean strength to toss the ball—is to let the weight of the ball do all the work. Let the ball actually push your arm out and down and through. It works every time; there is no margin here for failure. Too many bowlers are guilty of trying to muscle the ball. Brute strength is meaningless in bowling. Some of the best bowlers are skinny guys with arms like pipestems. Don't grab the ball and try to push it into the downswing. Do not carry the ball. This will only make for too many bad shots and that's just what we're trying to eliminate. When your swing and steps become second nature, you will have won much of the battle.

As for the backswing, you will soon find out that the pendu-lum motion you've brought into play will never—well, just about never—take the ball back past shoulder height. (It *shouldn't* go back farther than that point.) The more you ask your arm to do the more room you are allowing for error. In some instances a player will build his particular game around an exaggerated backswing, but those are rare.

Okay, let's backtrack now to the first movements you will make. And remember this point: as you stand motionless on the approach, with the ball held comfortably in both hands, the elbow of your bowling arm must be tucked in at the waist or hips and ball in line with your shoulder. When you get going, push the ball away from your body only about as far as that first short step you are taking. If you push it out too far, you'll find your swing is ahead of your steps; not enough and your footwork will be too far advanced. From then on the weight of the ball will take over, your arm will straighten out (it will

Getting set for the delivery—elbow tucked in close to the hip, palm of bowling hand turned slightly to the right

The pushaway—the ball goes out a few inches and then to the side

The downswing—as the left foot
goes out, the ball hangs almost
straight down

The backswing—the ball is at the end of its arc, the arm straight and no higher than the shoulder blade

The follow-through—sliding foot and ball have reached the point of release at the same time

Getting set for the release—elbow doesn't "break" until it passes the hip

Releasing the ball—note that the thumb comes out first

Getting that "lift"—fingers actually pull up on the ball to get it into a roll

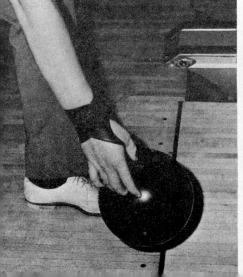

have to) and the elbow will remain locked in close to your body right on through the backswing, right on until the point where you lift the ball. This is where the elbow finally (it really is only a matter of a second or two) breaks away. This will occur approximately three inches past your hip. Now your arm and hand are ready to release the ball. Your forearm, from elbow to wrist, does the physical work now, lifting the ball up and out in the direction of the pins.

Putting the steps and stance and arm swing all together, it goes exactly like this: on the first short step, you go into your push-away—getting the ball in motion. Now you accelerate slightly. You have two steps to get the ball down and back and up to the zenith of the backswing. You've now gone through three steps. One step (slide) to go and one forward thrust of the arm. They must coincide or else you'll never get the consistency of delivery that is vital. Slide and the release motion must begin together. Work on it and get it down pat.

You can help your game immensely by practicing your footwork and arm swing, and you don't have to trek to the neigh-

Reach for the target area—don't simply get the ball into a roll and quit on the shot

borhood lanes to practice. Any time you have time and anywhere you might be will be adequate. Just do all the things
described—with or without a ball. What you are doing is trying
to get the movements so coordinated that before long they will
be second nature. If ever practice made perfect, this holds true
for bowling. A few minutes devoted to your armwork-footwork
will serve you well in future games.

Gripping the Ball

I'll get a bit more detailed about this aspect of bowling from
time to time, but right now you should learn something about
the insertion of your fingers in the ball—either as you move
into your starting position on the approach, or once you've
fixed your feet and locked your mind in on the job that lies
ahead.

Don't toss this one off lightly. A carelessly placed thumb,
or a finger or two that doesn't slip into the ball properly or
comfortably most definitely will affect your game. You certainly
wouldn't want to get up to the foul line perfectly coordinated
and as you get set to release the ball have that sickening feeling that comes from a faulty grip.

There are three basic grips, and when I speak of grips I'm
talking about the two holes where your ring and middle fingers
are inserted. They are called conventional, semifingertip, and
full fingertip. Which one is best for you depends on how comfortable a particular grip feels and at what stage of your bowling career you are in.

The conventional grip is suggested here for the bowler who
plays the game only occasionally. The sometime bowler will
find that this grip offers him the most consistency and will provide the proper feel. That's most important to him, for he's at
the stage where he wants his game to develop, not at a stage
yet where he seeks maximum action.

The semi and fingertip will stretch your span considerably
and as a consequence will impart much more hook to the ball
than will the conventional. What it also means is that if you
plunge right into one of the more refined fingertip grips, you

The end of the slide. You should come to a stop a few inches behind the foul line

The conventional grip—with thumb inserted first

Fingertip ball—with fingers inserted first

will have to start practicing more regularly than perhaps you had planned on so early in your development stage. It can be difficult to control a ball that hooks—for you—erratically.

If you have a conventional grip, place your thumb in first. Then place your two fingers into the ball. They'll go into the ball up to the second knuckle.

When you go to the fingertip grip, you'll note the difference almost immediately. The uppermost fingers will go in only as far as between the first and second knuckles, for the semi, only as far as the first knuckle on the full fingertip. In these instances, the fingers go in first, then the thumb. What the fingertip grip does is take away some of the strength in the ring and middle fingers and transfer it to the thumb.

Reviewing briefly, on a ball with a conventional grip the thumb goes in after the other two fingers are inserted. On a semi or fingertip grip, ring and middle fingers go in first, then the thumb. Please don't ever depart from this rule; it will take just a second or two longer to do it the proper way and the payoff will be in better bowling.

Let's move on now to how you want your fingers to be held once you've gone into the backswing and are ready to fire away. You've probably heard this one before and it still holds true. The thumb should be so positioned that it is fixed in a position that would be at nine or ten o'clock on the face of a clock. We'll even allow you eleven o'clock, but nothing beyond that. Once you get that thumb up at twelve and on top of the ball you run the risk of throwing a straight ball, or even one with a reverse hook; and you all know that good bowling never is achieved with anything but a ball that has spin on it as it careens toward the pocket.

It's true that some of the better bowlers do alter the position of their fingers on some shots, but that's a sophistication that will come when you learn how to "read" the lanes. For most of you, keeping the thumb in the nine- to ten-o'clock position keeps you in the safe zone and you'll be able to lift the ball from the side and get the right revolution on it.

Let's take a quick look at what will happen—most assuredly —if you allow your thumb to go counterclockwise, perhaps down to eight o'clock, or even seven. In this case you'll be *over-turning* the ball (if you ever listen to the pros talking you'll hear that expression come up quite often as they analyze what went wrong with a ball that seemingly looked perfect). Over-turning the ball will just make it spin and you'll wind up with "pocket splits," the bane of every bowler, amateur as well as pro. It can be tough enough at times getting that ball into the right area for a strike, only to see the eight and ten pins standing defiantly in an almost unmakable split. The ball "had nothing on it" and didn't do the job it started out to do. In plain language, you'll be getting bad reaction from the ball when it could have been eliminated easily.

As the ball is released, bear this in mind: the thumb always comes out first. There is no variation on this theme. The thumb always comes out first, a split second before the ring and middle fingers start doing their job. As the thumb comes out, and the elbow loses its rigidity, the fingers will actually lift the side of the ball (they hardly have a choice) and you'll get the right kind of revolutions on the ball. Many bowlers are guilty of following through with a straight elbow. You can't get the job done in the right fashion unless you start breaking the elbow as it passes the hip. Sound complicated? It really isn't. Give it a try and maybe you'll discover you've been doing it right all along; and if not, you'll quickly see how you are going to get that all-important lift when you allow your elbow to give and your thumb comes out of the ball first.

Here is one final point on the release, and this one is vital for in one respect it may refute everything you've ever heard. Instructors usually tell their pupils to "reach for the pins" as they let go. Well, the message here is to "reach for your *spot*." This variation is almost the theme of this book. It doesn't matter whether the target area is close or far out on the lanes. It's a spot for which you'll be reaching. Those pins sixty feet away can create what is sometimes referred to as the "straight arm illusion." This means that all too easily you can get into the habit of not breaking the elbow and you're following through with a straight arm. Learn to reach for your spot— your target area—and almost naturally you'll find your arm will do all the things it is supposed to do.

Being Thin Can Help

There are pros and cons to almost every facet of bowling— and this makes for interesting conversation whenever the bowling clan gathers on or off the lanes. One controversy is whether the lean, thin-hipped bowler has an advantage over the bowler who tends to be heavy and has a bit of bulge on the hips. There definitely is a relationship between narrow hips and better bowling.

During a recent National Championship of the Professional Bowlers Association, Don Johnson—one of the finest pros in competition today—made a statement regarding Jim Stefanich. Johnson is tall, loose-jointed, and narrow of hips. Stefanich, one of the finest pro bowlers of the day, isn't exactly overweight, but he's not as narrow through the hips as he'd like to be. Johnson said: "Jim's one of the best bowlers in competition today, but he'd be even better if he was built, say—like me."

With the stress put on keeping the elbow tucked in close to the waist on the backswing and follow-through, the wider the hips the more circuitous route the ball must take. You have to steer clear of the hip with your arm and elbow—that is, if you don't want to make a minor adjustment in your game. And, once again, I don't want you to change things unless you suspect your scores are not reflecting your ability. Here's what you can do if, perhaps, you're built along the lines of a Jim Stefanich.

Tuck your elbow in close to your hip and then turn the palm of your hand slightly toward the right to line up with your shoulder. Keep the ball lined up with your shoulder on all deliveries and never hold the ball right out in front of you. It will only mean that the wider your hip, the farther out to the right (or left, if you bowl that way) you must take the ball on the backswing and follow-through. This will create two bad habits all at once: the pros call it the wraparound and all it ever accomplished was to increase the chances of your pulling the ball, or "throwing it out the window"—meaning, you will propel the ball on an erratic flight, when it's a true arc you seek. If you're overweight, dieting may help. If you're wide-hipped and want to see if you can circumvent a problem, then try what has been suggested: elbow in, ball held in a line with your right shoulder.

Here's a final pointer on how you wrap up the whole stance steps-delivery picture. When you reach the point of release, always keep your wrist locked in. Make no attempt whatsoever to twist the ball or turn your wrist. Revolutions and lift power are created only by *lifting* the ball, not by turning it. Some of the pros turn and lift, but this boils down to a matter of split-second timing. If you are in the habit of practicing anywhere from seventy-five to one hundred games a week, as do many of the pros, that's just fine. If not, confine your release to keeping the wrist locked in. Turning the wrist does not apply a hook to the ball; the lift and follow-through alone create the revolutions you must have on the ball to get maximum pin action.

Spot Bowling

The bowler has a variety of devices and equipment to help him bowl better. Among the most important keys to good bowling are the arrows, or range finders, which are the lines of demarcation separating those thirty-nine boards I spoke of. Starting from the left, every fifth board is imprinted with a darker shade of wood. These are the guidelines for all better bowlers. Everything you have done behind the foul line will be meaningful only when you learn to hit the target area consistently.

Actually, spot bowling is a misnomer. The pros call their system "target" or, preferably, "area" bowling. The reason is that it is almost impossible to confine your shot to one board, or one arrow. Instead, the pros talk about hitting the 7-8 boards. Here is something you should know before we get into the intricacies of area bowling. Those two sets of dots you see on the approaches of every lane line up with the range finders. There's no variation in them. The first set of dots is twelve feet from the foul line; the second set is three feet farther back, fifteen feet from the foul line. Then there is one more foot before you run out of approach. If you need more room, perhaps you ought to forget bowling and take up pole vaulting. With the center range finder (there are seven, of course) fifteen feet away from the foul line, you will be some twenty-five to thirty feet from the middle arrow. At the foul line you may find another set of dots. These, too, are in line with the rear set of dots and with the range finders out on the lane.

In some bowling centers, whoever constructed the lanes for some reason eliminated the dots that would correspond with the first arrow on the right and the first one on the left. Or, in other words, there are five dots, the outside ones lining up with the second range finders. It can be confusing, but it will cause no problem.

Those are the vital statistics of those key dots and the arrows. Learning them will help you bowl better and make you a much more astute student of the game.

The approach area is usually sixteen feet long (note the dots, which will help you line up your shot)

Watch your line—dots at the foul line are in direct line with dots and range finders out on the lane

The only time you should actually look at the pins is to see which pins are standing should you be shooting for a spare. That's the only time.

The first time you went bowling you wouldn't be expected to plunge right into the area system of bowling; there are too many rough spots in your game that must be ironed out. But

The strike shot—sliding on the sixteen board, sending the ball out over the ten board

once you get into the swing of things, you should start to aim for the second arrow. It's the one used most commonly and is the one that will help you find the track (more about this later).

Each bowler has his own strike angle, however, when he goes to a house for the first time. It may be the tenth board, or the twelfth, or it may be as low as the eighth. Remember, we're talking about boards, one inch in thickness, starting from the extreme right side of the lane—with every fifth board an arrow or range finder. You cannot hope to get to be a really fine bowler until you learn to think, talk, and play the boards. It's not just happenstance that their width is standardized and that someone took the time and trouble to darken the wood of every fifth board.

Though there may be some variance in some of the older bowling centers, generally the lanes themselves are constructed

There are usually thirty-nine boards on each lane; the range finders (arrows) are located every fifth board

of maple and pine. Maple is the harder of the two woods, and it is maple on which your ball lands when it leaves your hand. A short way down the lane, the wood becomes pine, which is of a softer consistency. If a bowler comes into a house where he knows the wood is different from what he normally rolls on, he'll adjust accordingly. This should be of no concern, though; no doubt you do—and will be doing—your bowling on lanes made of maple and pine.

The "track" area could be somewhere between the seventh and thirteenth boards

The Track: What Is It?

It may appear that the lane on which you are bowling is as smooth as a plate of glass. Actually, it is not. During the course of a day, there will be many, many games bowled on any given lane, either by open bowlers or league competitors. This constant rolling of a ball causes a depression, called "the track" in the wood and in the finish that is applied over the wood. While a bowler always tries to find the track, sometimes even after he does he still has problems.

In practically every bowling center in the country, and on practically every one of the lanes the track will cover an expanse ranging from the seventh through the thirteenth boards —or seven to thirteen inches. That's the area where most bowlers set down their ball and start it toward the pins. The track most assuredly is a groove in the lane and the object is to find it and to narrow down a wide track to an area where you can zoom in on the pocket.

Once the track has been found, there remain several other factors to be considered. You're not just going to put your ball down in a furrow, place your hands on your hips, and then wait for all ten pins to lie down and play dead.

On the surface of all lanes there rests a layer of extremely thin oil; this dressing is applied daily to all lanes as a protective measure. The friction caused by a rolling bowling ball would soon gouge out each lane were it not for the dressing. Much depends, therefore, on where the oil has been applied—the procedures change from house to house—and how much oil has been applied. Then, too, there are atmospheric conditions to be considered; moist air or dry air will affect the lane, the same way that warm air and cool air will. Don't forget, what happens down at the pit end also depends on how much strike or hook power you have on your ball.

Finding the track is crucial if you hope to pump big numbers into your scoring, but do not lose sight of the other factors, all of which contribute to your carrying power when you hit the pins properly.

The thing to keep uppermost in your mind about the track

is that it can be both a benefit and a bugaboo to the bowler. If the lanes on which you are bowling have recently been resurfaced, then the track will be only a slight depression. When you find it, you'll be rolling on a true condition. That's what the pros are looking for—a flat surface, or one with very little depression. Better bowlers have so perfected their timing and armwork that they needn't be overly concerned with those aspects. What they then seek is a surface that will make their ball react truly. The flatter the surface, the truer will be the roll imparted to the ball.

When you are hitting a track from different angles, you can just imagine what may pop up on different shots. You'll possibly see your ball jump out of the track, or you could have the ball skip right by the track. No doubt there have been several instances when you've gone bowling, thrown a ball that looked absolutely strike-bound, and then saw with dismay that suddenly it seemed to stop rolling toward the pocket. You probably came out of the track, or missed it.

The track and the inconsistencies of the track are a source of no little concern to proprietors, as well as to bowlers. In all too many cases, where lanes have undergone a full season of league and open play, the track gets so pronounced and has so many variables to it that better bowlers sometimes are frightened off, or don't perform up to their abilities. A lane with poor tracks can make a bowling ball act almost as if it were riding rails going down toward the pocket. Bad boards can make bad bowling.

Left-handers often have a great advantage over the right-handers. There are far fewer left-handers and thus far less action on their side of the lanes. Hence, that track takes much longer to develop and is considerably less depressed than the right side. Left-handers have seized this opportunity to make merry. A good left-handed bowler, with a solid game on all counts, is going to be shooting on a flatter surface nearly all the time and can rely on his ball to describe a perfect arc to the pocket he's aiming for. He is getting an even and steady hook and consequently more carrying power.

An ideal corrective, at least insofar as a professional bowling tournament is concerned, is to have lanes resurfaced much more often than they are. The general rule was for a proprietor to resurface his lanes once a year, usually at the end of the league season, when there was a slackening of play.

The procedure is much like taking an old piece of furniture that has nicks and bruises upon it. All finish and oil are removed, as is the upper crust of the wood. There are several machines manufactured to do the job, but the essential process is sanding. All foreign substances are ferreted out and the wood underneath is smoothed. Then, new finish and oil are applied. If it were feasible for the process to be repeated much more often than it is, bowlers and proprietors alike would be much happier. But, the process cannot be done too often and the cost would be prohibitive.

Years ago, only tough lacquers and shellac were applied to the wood before the oil went on. These surfaces withstood all kinds of abuse and as a result a bowler wouldn't have to vary more than a board in any given day. The finishes of yesteryear held up so well that on almost every lane you would see a dark line develop from foul line to pocket.

Manufacturers in recent years have turned out products that are, in most cases, much different. Most of the finishes are plastic-based and react differently than they used to. The same holds true for the oil—or dressing—that goes on over the finish: the finish and oil break down more quickly than they used to. What promoted the changeover was a twofold projection: first, less maintenance for the proprietor, and second, a drier lane to enable the average bowler to get more hook on his ball. That it has worked is evident. Everyone—well, practically everyone —tosses a hook ball these days. But now all of us have to do much more adjusting than was once the case.

The way it is now, many pros must alter their game to the tune of two or three or more boards in one game alone. Many of today's bowlers—most of them right-handed—long for the good old days when surfaces were flat and no one over "threw a ball out the window."

The Bowling Pin

If you are to be the compleat kegler, you must know everything there is to know about bowling. The equipment you rent or purchase, the lanes on which you bowl, and the way you bowl are all part of the overall picture. But there is lots more, not the least of which is the pins at which you are shooting. The only good pin is a toppled pin, but there are quite a variety. They react differently, depending on when and where they were made, and of what they are made.

There was a time, almost in the days beyond recall, when all bowling pins were made only of wood. No other substance was used. But, just as almost everything else has undergone radical changes, so has the pin. And, with new manufacturing processes and new ingredients now going into the pin, it has opened the floodgates of controversy. Which, in a way, is good, because sports always seem to thrive on a difference of opinion and the viewing and participating public thrives on discussion.

A few years back it became increasingly difficult to obtain the kind of wood necessary for the construction of pins. At

An inside look at a modern bowling pin

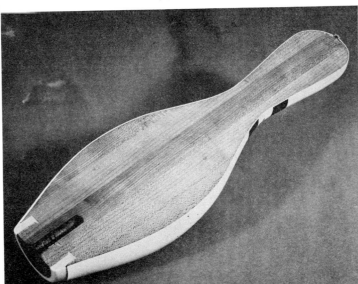

least, that's the way the story goes. So, new methods of manufacturing had to be found. What easier way than to substitute
something else. The bowling pin manufacturers still started
with wood, but then they began covering the wood with a
plastic shell.

The Fine Points

In recent years there have been extensive experiments involving a pin that has no wood in it whatsoever. This pin is
all-plastic and the intent is that one day all the wooden pins
will be phased out and their places taken by synthetics. It may
be that this day still is far off, for bowlers have been inured to
thinking (perhaps with justification) that no pin provides such
consistency as does the wooden one, even a wooden pin that is
shrouded in plastic. Wood pins score well and the bowler
doesn't live who will accept a substitute unless he knows it has
proved itself through long and arduous battlefield testing.

There are some who harbor the suspicion that a scarcity of
wood really doesn't exist and that all bowling equipment manufacturers are seeking a way to put a bit more life into the pins
than perhaps had existed. It's much the same as the arguments
that rage on and on about the lively baseball, or the curved
hockey stick. The only truths we will go into are those that
are evident.

In bygone days, the only substance that covered a bowling
pin was a veneer of lacquer. Today's pin, wood in the center,
is covered with plastic. There can be little quarrel from anyone that the pin does seem to have a bit more zip in it; the
resiliency factor is much greater. The plastic coating provides a
cushion for the ball on impact and as a consequence there is
more flying action.

Bowling proprietors may have had a say in determining a
change in the manufacture of pins. The plastic-covered pins are
easier to clean and maintain and there is one very strong point
in their favor, at least as far as a budget-conscious proprietor
is concerned. They last longer, because they can take much
more punishment.

In the long run, even though today's pins may be more expensive than they were at one time, the cost factor becomes negligible, for the pins have much more staying power. A set of ten pins will cost a proprietor anywhere from forty to fifty-five dollars. It may sound like a lot, but there are a lot of games in those pins.

Depending on several factors—climate, the condition of the automatic pin-setting machines, and maintenance—a pin will last from 2,500 lines (games) to about 4,500. The smart proprietor will remove pins from the machine about every one thousand games and service them. He'll have them cleaned, apply a thin coat of lacquer to preserve their looks and ensure their durability, and then reinsert them. By being this judicious in the handling of his pins—and, remember, there will be from eighteen to twenty in each machine—he'll lengthen their lives. The difference in showing big and small profits from a bowling center often will be predicated on the longevity of the pins used.

The plastic pin is most intriguing. There are several ways that the plastic is applied to the wood, each opening a new avenue of controversy. For example, there is one type of pin in which the plastic is not wrapped tightly around the wood, and a small amount of air space exists between wood and plastic. The bowler and proprietor alike agree that this causes problems in that each time a ball hits the pin the wood underneath gives a little—is depressed somewhat—while the resilient plastic springs right back to its original shape. Constant pounding on such pins eventually will widen the gap between wood and plastic so that much of its bounce, or flying power, will be lost.

On the other hand, there's the type of plastic applied to wood that reacts in a much different manner. In this case the plastic does not spring back to its original position after each impact. Instead, the plastic clings to the depressions in the wood and flying action often is enhanced. Two different pins, two different reactions, two different arguments.

Of significance is the way a pin reacts after it is hit by a bowling ball, or by another pin, or the way it ricochets off a side board is the weight of the pin and the way it is manufactured. While the specifications of a pin as to height and width are rigidly enforced, such is not always the case in how the weight of the pin is distributed. The proprietor has the option of ordering or purchasing pins that will do different things for different people.

The pin is made on a lathe and the manufacturer will turn out a hole in the middle. If his aim is to have a pin that will fly around much more, then he will shift weights accordingly. If he desires to produce a pin that will be more difficult to topple, than another set of weight-distributing rules is brought into play. Pins that create more flying action are perfect for the average bowler who loves to have someone or something give him any help he can get. Make no mistake about this part of the game— flying pins mean higher scores.

The bowling pin that the touring professionals shoot at almost always weighs in at three pounds, five ounces or three pounds, six ounces. The sets of wood are matched, meaning that there can be no more than a one ounce difference between any two pins in the rack of 18 or 20. The American Bowling Congress keeps a watchful eye on the mixing of pins, and it is their regulations that govern all bowling.

There have been, and still are, tournaments in parts of the country where the tournament director will have those entered shooting at pins that weigh about four pounds. You just know that the man wants to keep scores down so as not to discourage future entrants from trying to beat out someone with an astronomically high series. On the other hand, there are instances where two pounds, fourteen or two pounds, fifteen wood is used in tournaments and in leagues. That explains why you'll often see someone who has been averaging 195 or so in hometown leagues against only light wood enter a tournament with heavier pins and fall way down in average.

Should you or someone you know be fortunate enough to shoot a perfect game, a 300, a representative from the American Bowling Congress will visit the lanes forthwith and make a thorough inspection to see that all was in order. And, one of the things he does is impound the pins and weigh them out. If there is more than a one-ounce variation in any two, the 300 may be disallowed. It's not a bad practice for you to question your proprietor or his manager about the weight of the pins you are shooting at and to ask for assurances that they meet ABC specifications.

The wooden pin has gone the way of the fat-neck baseball bat and the nearly oval football. The oak, redwood, and other hardwoods that were used to make them are going into home construction and, perhaps, the construction of bowling centers themselves. Unless some proprietor somewhere isn't getting very much action on his lanes, or is holding the pins in his trophy room as keepsakes, forget about them. The name of today's game is plastic and that's the way it's going to be in the years to come.

Let the real old-timers of the game yearn for those days of yesteryear when only wooden pins were used and nary a pin ever flew up and away when it was struck. The manufacturing process today is much more refined, and a good healthy argument as to why this pin did this, or that pin did that, can only serve to generate even more enthusiasm among bowlers than now exists.

Maybe the pin is synthetic, but a very real fact is that there are more and better bowlers today, shooting under a staggering variety of conditions, than there ever were. And, standing in the wings, are millions of youngsters in junior programs who don't know a wooden pin from a wooden nickel—and wouldn't accept either of them.

3.

Spare Shooting

THE object of bowling, naturally, is to throw strikes. But no one ever reaches perfection in anything he does—not in business, certainly not in sports. In bowling, an integral part of the game is the second chance afforded all bowlers after they've failed to record a strike on their first shot. This is similar to missing a putt while out golfing, missing a pitch in baseball: you pay a penalty but get another chance.

Throughout your bowling career the likelihood is that you will not get as many strikes as you will chances to shoot once more for the spare. So it goes without saying that learning to shoot at spares, and learning the right way to make them, is vital if you are to become more than just an intermediate bowler. You'll be doing lots more adjusting and you will have much more on your mind when shooting for spares than you will when you step up to the line and try for strikes.

Initially, we should go into why all the pins do not fall down each and every time the strike ball goes right into the pocket, the one-three for right-handers, the one-two for left-handers. It will go a long way toward learning how to shoot for spares if we can find a logical reason why all the pins do not topple all the time. When we speak of "leaves" (pins left standing) we're writing for a predominantly right-handed society; the corresponding pin or pins on the other side would hold true for lefties. And it would seem only proper that the first discussion be about why the 10 pin stands on a perfect hit.

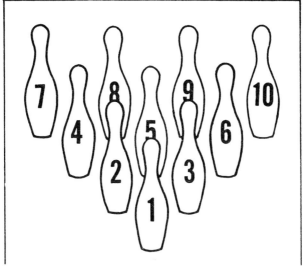

This is how a full rack of pins looks—and the way they are numbered

This is the 1-2 "pocket" the left-hander will shoot for. If a bowler tosses a backup ball, it will follow about the same path

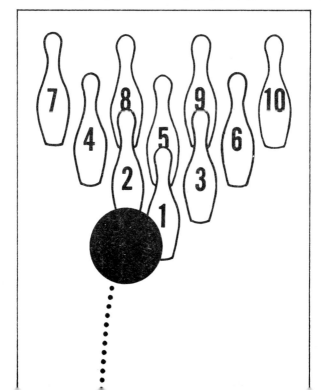

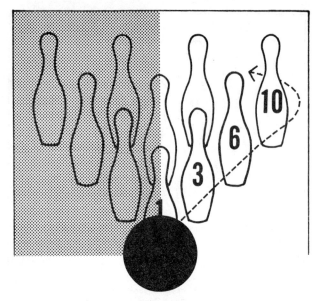

The "solid 10" or the "10-pin tap" occurs when the 6 wraps around the 10 instead of careening into it

The culprits always are the 3 and 6 pins, the ones we have to depend on to take out the 10 pin. When the 10 doesn't fall, the pros say they've been victimized by "the solid 10" or "the wraparound." It means that the aforementioned 3 and 6 have not done the job they must if a strike is to be posted. Then, too, there's the "weak" 10. Here, too, the 3 and 6 have failed. What has happened on this shot is that the ball actually has been driving into the pocket without too much velocity, and the proper deflection has not been achieved. The strike ball hits the 3 too solidly and sends it almost straight back, hitting the 6 a glancing blow on the left side. The 6 darts out almost at a right angle and falls short of the 10, again failing to do the job it should.

A variation of that shot—the one with too much drive—is what occurs when the 3 pin, which is hit by the ball, hits the 6 and sends it straight back. The 3 then glances to the right and wraps around the 10, instead of hitting it. This sounds a bit complicated, but it takes only a split second and there it is—a stubborn pin keeping you from that strike.

7

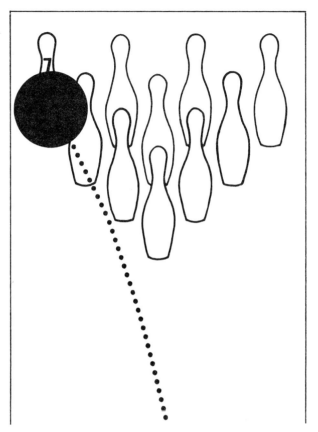

This is the path the ball would take if a right-hander was going for the 7. Of course, if it was a left-hander, it would be the same as a right-hander going for the 10

It's not an everyday occurrence, but often the 7 pin fails to fall on what appears to be a perfect hit. This happens in two ways, one of which is the "swishing" pocket hit, where the ball hits the 5 pin (which stands in dead center) a blow on the right side and sends it off to the left, often only to fall short of taking out the 7. You could also refer to that as the weak 7. On a more solid pocket hit, the 2 would go almost straight back, clip the 4, and then the 2 would go off to the left, only to stop in front of the 7. With today's variation in pins it often happens that the 2 pin, or any other pin for that matter, may even fly clear over the pin or pins it is supposed to fell.

A particularly frustrating thing that can—and does—happen to a bowler is to have the 5 remain standing on a good hit. Here again there are two reasons for this. First, the ball may have "rolled out," meaning that it has lost just about all of its oomph at the point of impact. Then, it is conceivable that the bowler has been playing a poor angle—not lined up properly on the approach before he let go with the strike ball. Let's dwell on the "half pocket" hit, for almost always that's the cause of the reluctant 5.

Sometimes the ball starts its revolutions much too early on the lane, on the "head," which is that area between the foul line and where the range finders are located. By starting its revolutions too early, the ball then has to use up practically all its hook power in trying to get back to the pocket. The pros would say that you're "bellying" the ball too much, making it go off in a direction that it shouldn't. Quite often the ball does get back to the pocket, but it has been shorn of its hook power to some degree and rolls out. Then it deflects too much, instead of driving deeply through the pocket, and this deflection often fails to include the 5 pin among the victims.

It may be that the bowler is playing "too deep a line" and as a consequence triggering the same poor deflection. The ball would drive into the headpin almost directly after failing to catch the track. Make no mistake about this: the 5 pin that refuses to go down can be traced directly to poor deflection among the pins.

A puzzler to all bowlers is the 8 pin. Or, rather, why it would not go down with all those other pins. Why, then, doesn't it fall? Here again the ball has come into the pocket with too much drive. The ball crashes into the 5 and sends it straight back past the 8 when it is the job of the 5 to take out the 8.

You'll hear the better bowlers talking about the solid 4

4 — 5

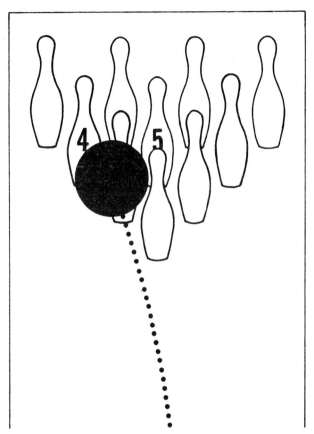

If you should leave the 4-5 split, take heart: there's room to fit the ball between them

and leaving the 4-9. They seem to go hand in hand and perhaps more than any other leave in bowling it's the 4 that drives bowlers mad. They can't comprehend why the 4 should remain erect on a good-looking shot. The 4 stands only because of a "high" hit—one where the ball hit a bit too much of the headpin. The headpin drives the 2 straight back and then continues on its way to the left, missing the 4 completely,

4 – 9

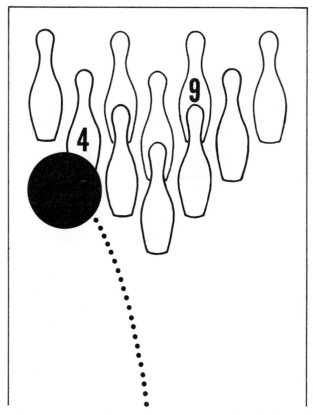

The 4-9 is a rather frequent split. You must hit the 4 lightly on the left side, sliding it into the 9

and knocking out the 7. It should be the 4 that takes out that rear pin but, obviously, the correct kind of chain reaction has not been set up.

Everyone of us has at one time or another—and often at a crucial juncture in league bowling—been perplexed and anguished at the "pocket split." It's annoying because it results after we thought we'd done the job perfectly, getting the ball into the 1-3 pocket. This one compares with what happened when the 5 pin was left standing; it's the result of too much deflection. The ball and pins cannot do the job correctly and pins that should have gone over do not. The pocket split is the 8-10 and it's almost unmakable. The 8-10 does have a cousin, however, and it's a kissin' cousin because you have a halfway decent chance of converting this one. This is the 5-7 and it, too, results from a ball that failed you somewhere along the line because you failed the ball behind the line.

Look at it this way and maybe you'll better be able to appreciate the assistance the ball needs down at the other end. Once the ball hits the 1-3 pocket, it can be expected to hit only two more pins before it falls into the pit to be returned to you. That's a total of only four pins—two of them after hitting the pocket. Those two are the 5 and the 9. You can readily see the margins for error when you consider all the variants—where the ball hit the pocket, the revolutions on the ball, the distance between pins (one foot), the kind of pins being used, the age and consistency of the kickbacks (side boards at pit end) and on and on.

A strike ball is a pretty wonderful thing, considering that it does so much in so short a space of time. Cherish your strikes and be more tolerant of the leaves. It'll help you be a better spare shooter.

An interesting-looking spare is the "washout," which is the 1-2-4, all on a slant, with the 10 pin tossed in for good measure (and to make this a difficult conversion). It happens when your ball does not get up to the pocket and instead barrels into the 3. The 3 goes straight back and the 6 wraps around the 10, instead of hitting it. The ball and other pins carry everything off, and left in their wake are those four pins. This is a makable spare and a satisfying one. Bad angle and a ball that didn't get up to the pocket are the causes of the washout.

There are unbelievable combinations of pins that may be left standing after the first ball, and excepting the washout, we have gone into only those leaves that have resulted from what appeared to be ideal strike balls. In the ensuing pages I shall tell you how to shoot these—and other—spares. That will be the section on "parallel lines," which is the essence of good bowling.

Without getting into the system too deeply, too early, keep this in mind as you contemplate how to convert any spare.

You will always use the same spot out on the lane for spare shots that you use on your first ball, the strike shot. You will

The object here is to hit the 5 pin lightly on the right side, sliding it into the 7

5 – 7

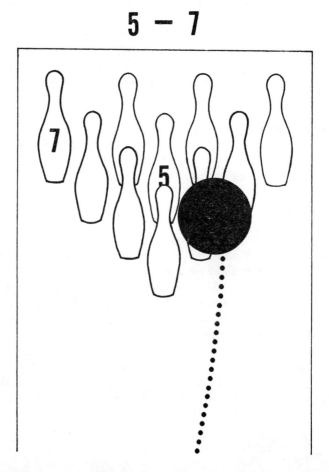

move only your feet to a different position, but never your mark or spot. The only deviation from that rule is when you go for the 10 pin. The golden rule to follow is that you always face your target: no turning sideways or slanting your head or body. Face the target squarely, point your feet toward your spot, and you'll be going a long way toward picking up those spares and being a much better bowler.

For some time there have been discussions among bowlers about whether or not to vary the speed of the ball on shooting spares. Some feel the ball should be thrown faster, some believe a slower ball is called for on second shots. The very fact that there is dissension would indicate that some rule should be established and followed.

Unless you roll seventy-five to one hundred games a week, you should never vary the speed of your shot. It's all right to get more sophisticated once you have an awareness of what you're doing. Always maintain your speed and you'll eliminate many a bowling problem born out of tinkering with your speed and timing.

Here's the chain reaction touched off on a strike hit

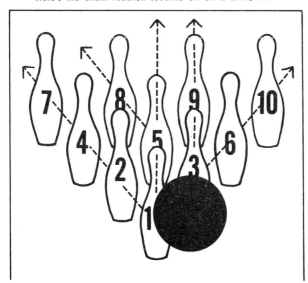

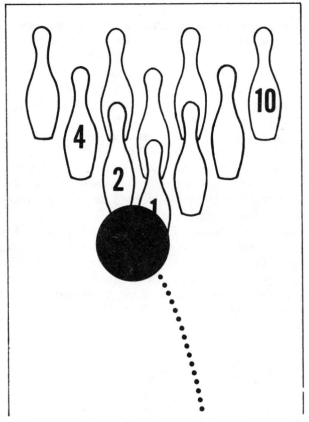

This is the "washout" and in order to pick up all pins you must hit the 1 pin on the left side and slide it into the 10. The ball will then hit the 2 and send it into the 4

There are certain spares on which I change my speed, because through the years I have experienced difficulty converting them unless I did. Rather than becloud the issue, they'll go unexplained. Many pros definitely speed up on their spare ball when they're shooting for the 10. That's to eliminate the possibility of the ball hooking too soon and going by the 10 on the left side. Remember, the 10 pin and all of those in the back row are three feet farther back than the headpin. You'll still be better off if you keep your speed the same throughout—for strikes and spares alike. Every time you start speeding up you must have a corresponding change in your arm swing and footwork.

Spare shooting never should be taken lightly, even though you have a greater margin for error in picking up, say, a single-pin spare than you do in trying for a strike. A missed spare all too often means the loss of a game or a championship. I recall an incident that happened some years ago in a big pro bowling tournament. It illustrates vividly, and sorrowfully, how being lazy in shooting spares, especially those spares you think are so easy, can be ruinous.

I had left a 10 pin after my first shot. All I had to do now was pick up the spare, make eight on the next ball, and I would be assured of a first-place finish. Well, I just casually went through the motions of making what ordinarily was for me an easy spare. I evidently eased up in the shot and the ball hooked away from the pin, giving me an open frame and costing me first place.

Spare shooting requires so much concentration that bowlers do themselves a disservice by not dedicating themselves to this part of the game more than they do. When you shoot for a tough spare like the 2-4-5-8, you have to place that ball almost perfectly, making sure it hits three of those pins. That's only one less pin to hit on your second shot than your strike ball does. Keep that in mind. It may help you hone in on your target more accurately next time.

Time and again the rule proves itself out in actual competition, or otherwise. You need only make all of your spares and just *two* strikes over the span of ten frames to ring up a 200 game. And that's what it's all about, isn't it? It's the missed spare—the split—the chop that gives you that 150 game and for every one of those you must have a 250 to get you back on the 200 beam.

The never-say-die method of bowling also works wonders. While the better bowler always goes for the one certain pin when he's confronted with a split that is rated as "impossible," there really is no such thing as an impossible shot in bowling.

I remember the time I was in an important competition some years ago. There it was, staring me right in the face—the 7-10, the most dreaded and "impossible" of all splits.

I knew I couldn't make that one by sliding one pin to take out the other, so I went for the sure one pin. I shot for the 7 and to my amazement it hit the kickback, came out of the pit and took out the 10 pin. I had made it and couldn't believe my eyes. Anything can be done, so never give up on a shot.

Watch the action in any handicap league and you'll probably see one spare shot at more often than any other. This is the 1-2-4 or the 1-2-4-7, both of which signify that the bowler didn't get his ball up the pocket properly. If you don't get at least a piece of that first pin there is no way you are going to get a strike. All too often the bowler tries to make an adjustment with his arm swing instead of doing it with his feet.

If the ball is not getting where you want it to go, it is mandatory to shift the position of your feet on the approach. You cannot—you must not—stay in the very same place on your next shot and think that, when you get up to the line to release your shot, you can make a correction with your arm. That's wrong and that's why you'll often see bowlers leave the 1-2-4 two, perhaps three times in a row.

Ask any bowler what spare he seems to be shooting at most and you'll get a ready answer. It's one of the conversation pieces of the sport. I have two of them that I seem constantly to be going for—the 4 and 10. Both of those leaves are the result of a sharply breaking ball. Since my early days, I have been trying to uncover a sure-shot method for avoiding the 4 and the 10. Some weeks it works, some weeks it doesn't. It depends strictly on what condition the lanes are in and what angle I'm playing.

The spare that gives me the most trouble is the 3-10, the baby split. Even though I have experimented with different angles and different speeds, I figure the conversions at 85 percent. And I'm not happy with that percentage, because— and this is an interesting statistic to remember—the pros bank on making 95 percent of their spares. That takes in splits such as the 3-10, for it is played exactly as you would shoot for the

3-6-10, with the ball glancing off the right side of the 3, into the 6, and on into the 10. On the 3-10, the ball hits the 3, glances off, and takes out the 10.

So while the pros are making 95 percent of their spares (including the baby split), I'm slightly below that figure, which is why the search for newer and better methods of knocking down pins goes on and on.

The proper way to get this spare is to put the ball between the 3 and 6. But you can also get it by hitting the 3 on its left side, sending it into the 6—which in turn will take out the 10

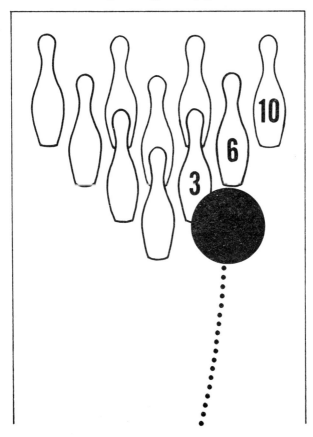

3 — 6 — 10

While we're still on spares and the psychology of shooting for them and the danger involved, here's a little note that will indicate just how the pro differs from the average bowler in forever trying to come up with solutions to vexing problems.

The professional bowler, knowing that in order to improve his game he must remove the shrouds of mystery that sometimes envelop various facets, has come up with a new and interesting method. He will watch the flight of the ball, of course, but after it has hit the pins, he will note where the ball has gone off into the pit area. Lower-averaged bowlers are intent only on seeing which pins remain standing.

By following the ball all the way, the bowler can see just where it drops off and thus he can tell just how much deflection there was on any given shot and can come up with a logical reason for why he must now shoot for a spare instead of having rung up a strike.

The good bowler knows that on a perfect pocket hit, with the right kind of "stuff" on the ball, the ball will plow into the 5 pin and then glance off to the right and take out the 9. If the ball is driving heavily into the 5, it may take the 9 out at a different angle. This isn't exactly bad, but the pro wants to know just how his ball is reacting on pocket hits and will observe carefully whether the ball drops off to the left of the 9 or to the right.

It goes without saying that much can be learned by never taking your eyes off the ball from the start of its flight until you can see it no longer. An adjustment can be made—a proper adjustment, that is—only when there is no doubt as to why a certain spare was left. Next time you go bowling, you might find it most rewarding to try this little ploy: watch the ball until the very end.

Naturally there are certain mysteries surrounding the leaving of certain spares and the failure sometimes of converting them. Just such an incident involved Dick Weber, one of bowling's all-time greats. It occurred on a television show some years back and cost Dick the championship.

On his strike ball, Dick left the 4-7 standing—a rather easy spare to convert. All you have to do is find your spot on the approach, send the ball over the right board, and if you hit the 4 pin it's a lead-pipe cinch that you'll also get the 7. Well, it didn't exactly happen that way. Dick's shot rolled smack into the 4 pin and then continued straight back instead of continuing its roll into and through the 7. How did it happen? Well, in the case of Dick Weber there are two reasons why it happened, considering the nature of his game. Dick's game is to get speed on his ball, and on his spares he'll usually try to cut down on his hook. He can do that because, as stated previously, he will generally shoot some one hundred games a week and is allowed some refinements in his game.

No doubt on Weber's try at the 4-7, he sent the ball down the middle, which he will do on those spares. And probably there was a lot of oil on the left side of the lane. His ball just plowed into the 4 and then went straight back, instead of maintaining its course toward the 7. It has to be one or both of those reasons—too much oil and Dick's speed. His ball didn't grab the lane in the right fashion. It is highly unusual for this to happen, but strange things do happen out on the lanes and your adjustments must be made in your mind as well as with your feet.

Shooting for spares can be exasperating, but it is also satisfying. The bowler has not been made who will always be philosophical about not having made a strike on what he "just knew" was a strike hit. But you've never seen a bowler disgusted with himself when he knew he needed a last-frame spare and got one even after his first ball looked to be a perfect strike and wasn't.

Until you learn that spare shooting is an integral part of bowling and until you accept the fact that not every "perfect" hit will knock down all the pins, bowling will be a struggle. And now that you've started making an adjustment in your attitude—assuming you needed one—suppose we start revealing just how you go about stationing yourself on the approach so that you'll minimize the chances of making a mistake.

4.

Parallel Line Bowling

THERE have been several earlier references to the construction of the lanes, to the boards. I have stated that the nature of your game and the kind of bowler you are and will become depends very much on how you learn and adapt to the only system of bowling that comes closest to guaranteeing a repeating shot. That's what the aim is in bowling and in all sports—being able to repeat, almost flawlessly, the same motion—providing, of course, that the motion is the correct one.

Let's venture into the most exciting aspect of our game, the one called "parallel line" bowling. In the pages that follow you will learn how to place your feet, how to zero in on your target, and how to make adjustments when necessary. It is this last factor that you will have to invoke most of the time, for there are so many different shots you will be called on to make and there are so many fluctuations in and on the lanes you bowl at that adjusting is not a sometime thing. It is an intrinsic part of bowling. With certainty, it is vital that you take the time to learn how to adjust properly if you are to take your game to the next level.

Through parallel line bowling you will learn how to line up for the strike and spare shot and a simple method for picking up all spares. You will discover various ways to play different angles and no longer will you be fearful of making the alterations in your game that once seemed so reprehensible.

With bowlers coming in so many different varieties, it would be senseless to make one hard-and-fast rule as to where they should stand on the approach and where they should release that first ball. What we want to do is "personalize" some of the rules for you to follow. So here's what you do first, so that we can determine just where you should start lining up, which boards shall be your guidelines.

You wouldn't want to start your experimentation during league play, or when the bowling center you frequent is crowded. Pick a time of day when the action has tapered off and take yourself and a sheet of paper about four feet square to a corner of the place.

Take the sheet of paper and place it three feet over the foul line, alongside the gutter, or channel, on the right side. Then get a few pieces of tape and affix the paper to the lane so it will not slide or shift position. Assuming that you are a right-handed bowler, find the correct distance (for you) from the foul line (I told you how to do that in Chapter 2) and place your left foot squarely on the center dot. That's the dot that is lined up with the center range finder out on the lanes, one of the seven you will see on every lane.

Make certain there are no pins set up at the other end. You are involved here in seeing where you generally would be dropping the ball on its way toward the pocket, not how many pins you can hit. Not yet.

Now, face your target directly, walk a straight path as you go through your delivery, and you will be dropping the ball on the four-by-four sheet of white paper. Repeat this about eight to ten times and you will see that a black mark has been left on the paper each time you've tossed the ball. Now I can analyze what you've done and help you determine a starting position on the approach. That's where good bowling begins. Remember that the arrows on the lanes and the sets of dots at the foul line and those farther behind are all in a line.

If you have slid correctly, in a straight line from your starting points, probably you are releasing the ball in an area anywhere from five to nine boards to the right of your left foot. The imprint on the paper will confirm or refute this, unless your path to the target area has been erratic. Once you find out how far to the right you release the ball from your original starting position (don't forget, there are thirty-nine boards in all, with every fifth board an arrow or range finder), you can forge a system for yourself on all ensuing balls.

If you are regimenting your footwork and arm swing, you will forever be following a pattern where you will shoot the ball over a board that is just about six boards (or six inches) to the right of where your left foot was stationed. Putting it another way: If you plant your left foot on the approach on the six-teenth board, and if you slide along the sixteenth board, you'll be shooting the ball over the tenth board, six inches to the right of where you stood. If your desire was to play "ten to ten" on the release, it means you'd be putting the ball down on the tenth board at the foul line and seeing the ball go out over the tenth board (second arrow).

To this point I have dwelt on the "six board" pattern. You may discover that your range is seven or eight or even nine boards to the right of your left foot. You will determine that soon enough by the marks on the paper. For clarity's sake, we are concentrating on six boards.

For the system to work—and I cannot stress this point too much—everything must be coordinated. You must stand at the right spot, walk a straight line, slide on the same board from where you started, and have your arm swing perfectly grooved. All factors are interrelated, and if one is wrong, no doubt you will pay the price on release.

If something is happening that is not to your liking, how would you adjust? It seems reasonable to assume that the most bothersome circumstance of all is that your ball is getting up to the headpin, but then comes in too heavily, too high. What should you do back on your end of the lane? Whenever the ball is moving to the left, your adjustment must be made to the left—meaning that if you are coming in too high on the head-pin, you know instantly that you have to shift to the left. Were your ball not getting up to the pocket, you'd be deficient to the right and as a consequence move to the right. That's the rule: always favor the way the ball is going. What you are trying to do is give your ball the best possible angle, thus giving it the best hitting power.

If you are playing "ten to ten" trying for the strike, and are standing on the sixteenth board, a change is dictated. If you are coming up only about one inch high in the pocket, you certainly should not make a radical change. What you will—and should —do this time is line your left foot up on the eighteenth board and play "eleven to ten," allowing for about six boards to the right. Your aim here is to get the ball to "belly out" one board from the eleven at the foul line to ten at the range finders. By allowing a one-board margin to the right of what originally was a high hit, presumably you will come in three boards lighter and presumably get a strike. But only if you do everything else right.

If you've been reading carefully, you've noticed that there was a deviation in the paragraph above. It's the way I sometimes make adjustments and it's the way I recommend that all bowlers amend their game when they have to. In trying to eliminate a high hit, you were told to forget the "ten to ten" and instead play "eleven to ten." But while you were making a one-board adjustment on the release, you were moving *two* boards to the left, from sixteen to eighteen. It's the way I do it and the way I want you to do it. Remember the rule—it's an excellent one and will work wonders with your game: for every one-board adjustment you make out on the lane, you make a corresponding *two*-board adjustment with your left foot. Then walk toward your target.

Naturally, the same rule should be applied in making adjustments to the right. It was only because the situation I described called for coming in less high on the headpin that I spoke of moving to the left.

Now, let's suppose that we make the adjustment we thought necessary on that high hit and we still come up too solidly on the headpin. Now what? Well, we just go right into another correction. This time we are going to play "twelve to ten," which means putting the ball down on the twelfth board at the line, bellying it out two boards to the right over the tenth board and hoping then that the ball will come in perfectly. What do we do with the left foot here?

Because we are now giving the ball a two-board belly, we add six boards from the release board (twelve) plus two for the belly, and find that we have to plant the left foot on the twentieth board. Bringing the rule up to date now, it's six boards to the left of where we put the ball down, plus the amount of boards we want the ball to go out (belly) before coming back in again. (We don't assume that everyone has the same width foot, or shoe, so a general rule to follow as to where to place the left foot on the dots is to have the board line up with the instep or heel. You'll make no mistake if you adhere to this practice.)

While it is of such importance that the left foot be properly placed, and that the dots and arrows be utilized so that they will help you improve your game, the right foot plays a placid role. It should be of little concern to you where it is placed, for most likely you will put it in a comfortable position. The pros recommend that the right foot be quite close to the left so that your weight will be distributed evenly, but you need not conform. You can keep your feet slightly apart—as many pros do—and find that it will have no bearing on the parallel line system; mainly, select a comfortable stance.

Once a bowler has passed from the intermediate range into better leagues and better scoring, he'll never deviate from the pattern that has got him that far. A bowler going into a strange (for him) bowling center does, however, need some guideline to help him through his first few shots. After all, the lanes of the country are like people's faces—no two are the same. What a bowler should do with his first shot is line up at sixteen and shoot out over the second arrow (the tenth board). Almost always that tenth board is just about where the track is located and before long he'll be able to chart his own course.

The track generally ranges from the seventh to thirteenth boards, so by playing down number ten he's just about splitting the track and finding the most pleasurable route toward the pocket. To be sure, the right-handed bowler knows he'll be in the ideal area, even if he hasn't found dead center of the track.

If you want to know how I do it, here's how: The first time I play a lane in tournament competition, I always put the ball out on a straight line over the twelfth board. No belly yet.

5 — 10

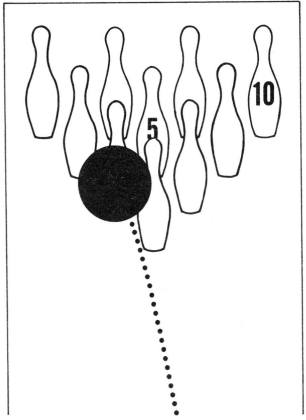

To get the 5-10, you must hit the 5 on the left side and send it over into the 10

And because I always stand six boards to the left of where I aim the ball, my left foot is fixed at the eighteenth board.

Let's tie some of those loose ends together, so you'll have a clear picture of what to do the next time your ball is not getting into the strike zone. First, you must get a mind's-eye picture of how high or how light is your hit. If you calculate that it's one inch, move your starting foot—your left—to the left if you're getting high hits, to the right if you're getting light hits. For a one-inch adjustment on the lane, move two inches on the approach. That's all there is to that. That's how you relate the parallel line system to strike shooting, and that's how you will always do it. No deviations, no estimates.

Now, let's apply the system to spare shooting. Here you will be faced with an almost endless variety of positions. On your strike ball, you're shooting for only one specific area. There's no telling what spares you'll be going for during the course of a day or a season.

Let's start with a pin or pins that are left standing in the center of the lane. This can be any combination of pins involving the 1 or 5, both of which are located on a line with the dots on the approach, the dots at the foul line, and the middle arrow. They're all treated the same, which is to say that you would want to duplicate the strike ball to topple them—a strike ball, that is, that is dead on target. Those pins might be the 5 all by itself, or the 1-2, or the 1-2-4, or the 1-2-4-8. The headpin standing by itself is a rarity, but the 5, located two rows behind it, directly behind, is one you'll be dealing with quite often.

Use the dots on your approach. Here's a shot with the instep of the sliding foot running parallel to the twenty-two board

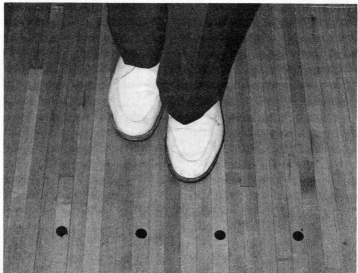

You haven't forgotten how often it stands on what appeared to be a perfectly thrown strike ball.

Assume the strike stance and go through the strike delivery, only this time do it the right way. If you were standing at sixteen and releasing on a "ten to ten" angle and failed to reach the headpin, you could move over two boards to the right (fourteen) and send the ball out over the nine to ten board on

When going for the 7 pin, move to the right and face the target squarely

6 — 10

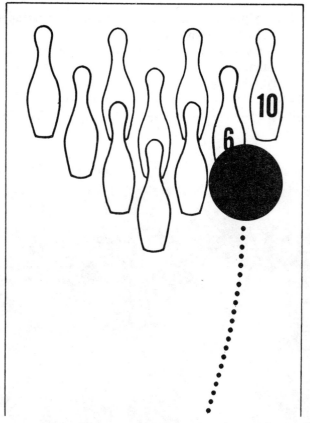

This is the route the ball should take to get the 6 and 10

a direct line to the pocket. Keep in mind that if you intended to belly the ball out one extra board you'd compensate by moving two boards on the approach.

Suppose you are playing the second arrow (ten boards from the right), which means you were standing on the sixteen board with your left foot, and you left the 4 pin or the 7 pin or both. How do you adjust for your second shot? You would shift ten

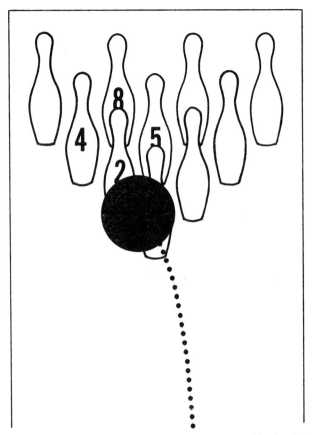

This is known as the "bucket," and the ball must hit the 2-5 pocket squarely to get all four pins to fall

boards to the right, putting your left foot instep on the sixth board. Now you'd position yourself, face your target, go into your delivery, and put the ball smack over the second arrow, the same one you were using on the first ball. The ball, if you've thrown it properly, will cross over the lane and take out either or both of the pins, if you've left both.

Perhaps you have left the 6, or the 10, or the 6-10 on your

2 — 4 — 5

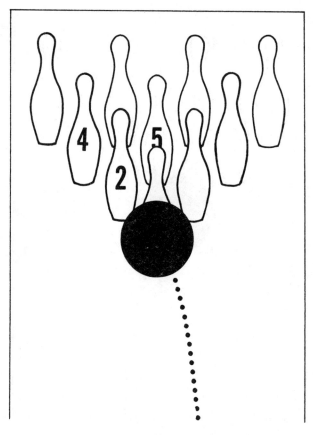

Always tough is the 2-4-5. The ball should hit between the 2 and 5—or, if you are left-handed, between the 2 and 4

first ball. The procedure is reversed. Because you were standing on sixteen and are now after a pin or pins on the right side of the lane, you would move ten boards to your left, to the twenty-sixth board, and still put your ball out over the second range finder. It's that simple and it works magic when you don't deviate from the master plan.

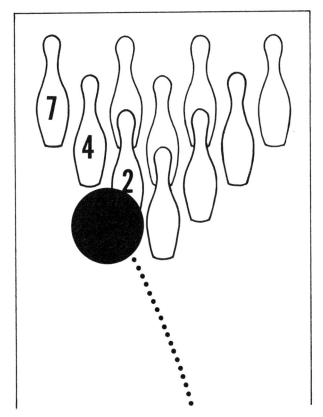

Put the ball between the 2 and 4 and the 7 will topple, too

What about any spare that involves the 2 pin? Of course, it may be the 2 alone, the 2-4, the 2-4-5, or the 2-4-5-8. The last two named are called the "bucket" and can be tricky. But if you adhere to the established rule, you'll make more than a fair share. Move five boards over to the right of where you stood for the strike ball. Then, you simply cross the same target

2 – 7

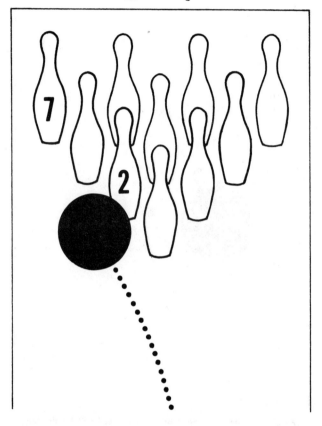

The 2-7 is the "baby split" for the left-hander, but on some occasions these pins are left standing by a right-hander as well. In any case, the object is to nick the 2 on the left side, after which the ball will deflect into the 7

area, which in this case was the second arrow. Do not forget, we are using the second arrow only for illustrative purposes. You would send your ball out on the second shot over any target area that you were playing.

Were you to leave the 3 pin or a combination of pins in-

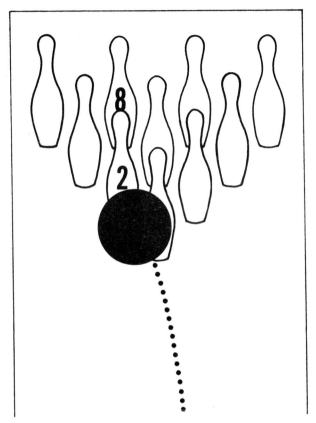

They sometimes call this "hidden wood." What this requires is a ball thrown straight on the pin in front, driving it into the pin behind. Variations of this spare are the 3-9 and 1-5 (although the last is a rarity)

volving the 3, the stance is reversed on the approach. Now you would move five boards over to the left and still shoot for the same target. If it's done properly the 3, 3-5, 3-5-6, and 3-5-6-9 will present no problem.

The only time you would make a change in this system

3 — 5 — 6 — 9

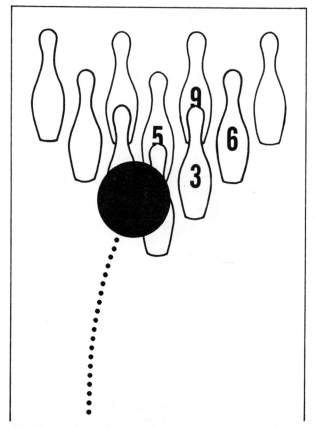

This is the "bucket" as the left-hander would see it. The object is to get the ball between the 3 and 5

would be if you were going after the 10 pin. Located at the extreme right, and just near the drop-off point of the pin deck, it requires a special stratagem. To get the ten, change the target five boards. If you were playing for strikes over the second arrow, you'd shoot for the ten by going over the third arrow,

When going for the 10 pin, move to the left and send the ball out over the third range finder

10

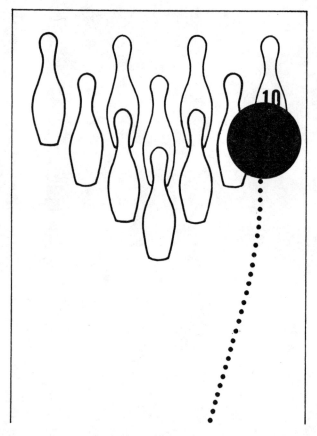

The 10 pin is regarded as a tough one by right-handers—and it is, unless you stand to the extreme left on the approach and send the ball out in this manner

five boards closer to the center. Of course, you would use that same board adjustment on the approach, remembering always to walk toward that target. This point cannot be emphasized too many times. Face your target and walk toward your target. It's the secret of parallel bowling.

How would you tackle that spare I spoke of just a little

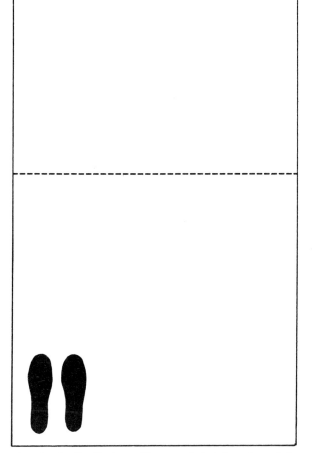

In going for the 10 pin, position your feet at the extreme left side of the approach

way back, the 1-2-4, sometimes referred to as the rail? With the 2 and 4 standing to the left of center, it would mean that you should aim a "Brooklyn" strike, or a ball that crosses over from the conventional 1-3 pocket and instead strikes the 1-2 pocket. I suggest that the bowler move two boards to his right and then send his ball out over the original target. You can pick

up this spare by playing another conventional strike ball—that
is, by hitting the 1 pin solidly on the right side and sending it
crashing into the 2, which in turn would fell the 4. But this can
be dangerous. Much better to have your ball go in between the
1 and 2 and have the 2 take out the 4.

The 3-10, or the baby split, as it's commonly called, requires a ball that will hit the 3 on the right side and then glance
off and take out the 10. Instead of honing in on a blank space,
imagine that the 6 pin stands smack in between the 3 and 10.
If you were shooting for the 3 (or any combination) I suggest you move five boards to the left and aim at the second
arrow. But since you really want to "hit the 6" you would go
two more boards to the left. Throw the ball well and the ball
will topple one imaginary 6 pin and two very real ones.

Though old-time bowlers probably used the parallel line
system—they may have called it something else—it really did
not come into vogue until about six or seven years ago. Years
ago, bowlers often would not divulge secrets to one another.
Today's players help each other more. I have tried to take the
parallel line system and make it apply technically and arith-
metically. Most better bowlers and professionals now use the
parallel line system in one fashion or another. They may use a
three-to-one ratio in adjusting, rather than the two-to-one recommended here, but that depends strictly on their own brand of
game. The important thing about this form of bowling is that it
gives the bowler somewhere to go; he doesn't have to second-
guess; he doesn't have to stand in the same spot and trust to
luck or a fickle judgment. The movements involved are so simple and so basic that each and every spare becomes almost fun
to shoot at. There is no second guess involved and the bowler
knows that no longer does he have to stand in the same spot on
the approach to shoot at all spares. With the lane over three feet
wide, it hardly makes sense that the bowler should be confined
to an area of just a few inches sixty feet away.

Everything you do, all moves you make, revolve around
your strike target, that area out on the lanes where you want
your ball to cross. Once again, this reminder: We have used
the second arrow for simplification, but this may not be the best

1-2-4 & 1-2-4-7

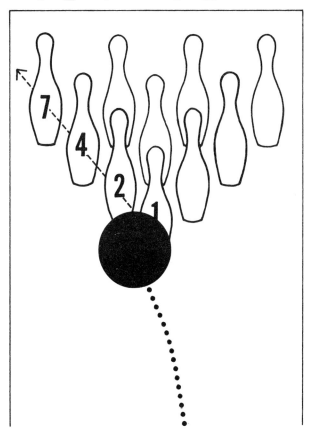

Whether it's the 1-2-4 or the 1-2-4-7, the ball should be directed toward the 1-2 pocket

shot for you. The strike target you play, though, is the same guide you will use on subsequent shots. Find the target area that is best for your purposes, always face the area squarely, and you'll be on your way.

Parallel line bowling ensures the bowler a free and easy swing at all times because it eliminates the necessity of making adjustments in the arm swing to allow for the ball taking a

3 — 10

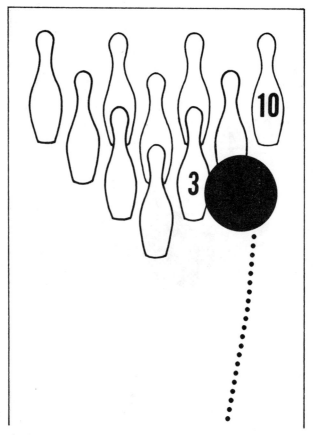

This is the "baby split" and to get it you should aim for an imaginary 6 pin. The ball, if tossed perfectly, will nip the 3 on the right side, then deflect into the 10 pin

different direction each time it is tossed. The bowler no longer has to pull the ball or loop it or corrupt his swing as he tries for a strike or spare. Movements become so simple that the only item the bowler need concentrate on is grooving his arm swing.

When you go bowling in the future, you have only to retain

4 — 7

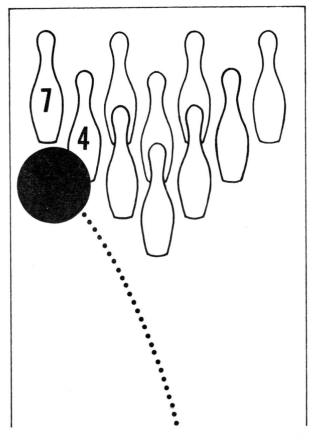

The 4-7 is an easy one, providing the ball is directed smack into both pins. Don't try to get this one by hitting the 4 on the right side

this message: In parallel line bowling you are attempting just about all the time to put your ball down on a board right over the foul line and having it cross a corresponding board at the point on the lane where the arrows are located. You will depart from that formula only when you occasionally belly the ball out a board or two when conditions dictate.

To sum up, here's a general pattern to follow in utilizing the parallel line system for making your spares. It's probably the single most important guideline for you, so pay heed:

On all spares involving the 4 (where the 4 is the pin in the forefront, such as the 4-7) and on spares involving the 6 in the same fashion, the adjustment is ten boards. On spares involving the 2 and 3, the adjustment is five boards. And, in each in-

This is a tough one—the 6-7. Even though the numbers are close, the pins are far apart. Here, too, you must nick the 6 on the right and slide it over into the 7

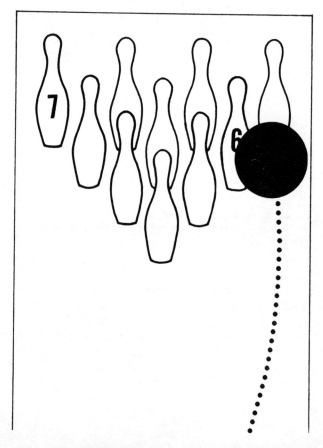

stance, naturally the adjustment is made either to the right
or left. As far as the 2 and 3 are concerned, they would include
the 8 and 9, which are located behind those pins respectively.

From now on, uppermost in your mind will be this fact:
You are putting the ball down at a point just beyond the foul
line, hoping that the ball will cross a board on the same line
when it reaches the range-finder area. You will swerve from
that predetermined course intentionally a few times, but basically it will be your intent to play the parallel line.

You cannot expect the ball to do tricks. With a skid involved
before the ball starts its hooking action, you would not expect
the ball to be able to go too far out and then start its way back.
If the lanes are extremely dry, you may find that the ball can

Picking up spare pins down the middle—slide on the fourteen board, send
ball out over the nine-ten board area

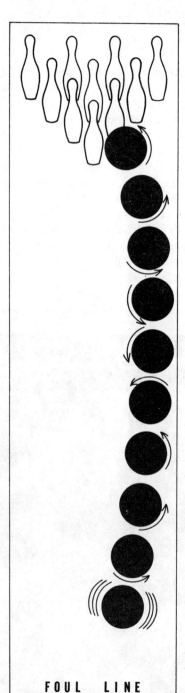

Once the ball has completed its skid, it will take about eight or nine revolutions before reaching the pins

FOUL LINE

belly out a few boards. There have been times when excellent bowlers were called on to lay the ball out a bit farther than usual, but they were able to read the lanes properly and decided that the ball could go out that far and still get back.

To understand better what goes on once the ball leaves your fingers, be aware that no bowler is able to impart an instant hook to the ball. There must be a skidding action initially and where the skid ends and hook begins will depend largely on how much oil has been applied to the lanes, and how deep the track may be. How many revolutions the bowler gives to the ball and how much hook power are also factors that have to be taken into consideration. In the final analysis, the friction of the revolution must overcome the force of the slide.

The minimum revolutions a ball will have are in the neighborhood of six, with a maximum figure being fifteen. If you are talented enough and have learned enough to get about nine or ten revolutions on the ball before it reaches the pocket area then you are doing quite well. But where the skid stops and break begins depends on the lane condition. It could be anywhere from twenty-five to forty feet out on the lane.

There may be an assortment of names given to the system just described, but just about all the pros are parellel line bowlers. If they're not, when they come out on the tour of the Professional Bowlers Association, they soon adapt to the system, for they see how it helps them. And even though not all fellows who try the tour fare well enough to remain out for any length of time, most of them go back to the towns and lanes where they started and become very competent instructors. It goes without saying that you can be a fine teacher of bowling and the parallel line system without being able to make your living from professional bowling. A dividend being paid to the bowling community is the abundance of fine junior bowlers being turned out by these instructors, who have brought the message home to the kids.

Line up properly, walk toward your target (don't ever look at the pins, except to see which ones are left for a spare) and learn how to adjust. That's all there is to it.

5.

Lane Conditioning

A bowling center represents a sizable investment. It is good business sense, financially as well as ethically, for the proprietor to be rigid in caring for everything that goes into the construction of a center. The cleanliness of the place is vital if it is to attract people, and maintenance of machines that set pins is crucial. Pins must be serviced and replaced and equipment that is loaned or rented to bowlers must be in perfect shape. Everything, though, diminishes somewhat in importance, at least as far as the bowler is concerned, when compared to conditioning—or dressing—of lanes.

Friction, the single factor that contributes most to automobile breakdowns, is also an ever-present factor in bowling. The constant roll of that bowling ball would quickly reduce the wooden lane to splinters and chips were it not for the care given each lane by the proprietor. Such care cannot be haphazard. In almost every center, oil—or dressing—is applied to all lanes for much the same reason you put oil in your auto's crankcase: it inhibits wear and tear.

It is the application of this dressing, however, that makes the game of bowling the intriguing endeavor it is. How the oil is put down, and where it is put down, and when, and its thickness, and the way the lane is polished (buffed) after its application are vital factors in the bowler's performance. If you are to remain a good bowler, or if you have your sights set on becoming a better one—perhaps a professional—you should know some of the methods used in lane conditioning. If you have never learned to "read" the lanes you just don't have a chance at bettering your game.

It goes without saying that there are many, many variations as to when and how the lanes are dressed. The proprietor first must read his charts and make determinations. If a block of lanes is hardly ever used for league action he would not have to oil the lanes as often or apply very much oil when he does. Open bowlers (ones who are not committed to weekly competition) do not "take that much out of a lane." So on those lanes that are used constantly by leagues, the application is daily and heavy. Were this not so, the wood would "burn."

Suppose the proprietor hears frequent rumblings from some bowlers that they are finding it impossible to make their ball hook. He has to have a different battle plan. He knows that newcomers to the game often do not care as much about how high their scores are as how much they are able to impress their friends by how wide a hook they can toss. Those bowlers, too, must be obliged, so the conditioning process takes on still another look.

In these instances the oil would be applied in such a manner as to leave those portions of the lane that the novice bowler

This is an AMF lane conditioner

Here's an AMF lane conditioner dressing (oiling) a lane

rolls on drier, thus allowing for the ball to grab quicker and better and allow for a hook.

Almost always the oil is applied by machines that do the whole job. The machines generally have a meter on them which can be set to put down a coat of oil at a specified width and length. The brushes that spread the oil are tapered and usually are made of nylon. The tapering means that the coat of oil set down is a trifle heavier in the center than it is near the channels (gutters). To visualize the area that receives a lighter coat, let us say that it is about an area of five boards at each side (five inches).

The oiling machines, the lane dressers, whatever you choose to call them, start the process just over the foul line and depending on how the man in charge dictates that the oil be spread, the area that receives the dressing will be from twenty to forty feet beyond the foul line. No oil is applied beyond that point (forty feet) as a general rule, but that is not to say that no oil gets out there close to the pins (sixty feet from the foul line). The bowling ball will pick up oil on its constant path to the pins and deposit some further than the point where the machine stops putting it down. To the better bowler this is an important factor as he goes about "reading" the lanes.

In that twenty- to forty-foot area the ball will be in its skid, for it is virtually impossible to get it to start its hook when it's on a slick surface. The alert bowler soon determines how far out the oil goes and just when to expect his ball to start hooking toward the pocket.

While most centers utilize a machine to put the oil on the lanes, some stick to the old-fashioned method of applying the oil to a mop and then putting it on the lanes with a buffing motion. Oil applied in this manner often lasts much longer than oil released by a machine and then spread with brushes. The choice is up to the proprietor, and the bowler who is keen will know the difference. The machine-buffing process (the buffer goes to work right after the front part of the machine spreads the oil) can be worlds apart from hand oiling and buffing.

Even this buffing procedure has its variations, and bowlers may want to know which way it was done so they can plan their game accordingly. The buffing can be done either from side to side or lengthwise. Hand buffing practically always goes from gutter to gutter, while the machine polishing process goes down the lane in the same direction as the boards.

Where an establishment has much play by women, either in leagues or open play, the lane conditioning process usually follows a pattern. The dressing will be set down only about twenty feet from the foul line. Women do not get as much hooking power as men and consequently the ball will not bite into the lane as much, and not require a protective film as often. Also, with the oil not that far out, the hook the woman does have on the ball will get a little boost from the dryness out closer to the pins.

With only about one out of every ten or twelve bowlers in the country being left-handed, the dressing strategy naturally takes this into account. More right-handed bowlers means more play on the right side and that means more oil on that side of the lane. You can see, therefore, that practically every bowling center in the nation must "custom dress" their lanes. It is just this inequity in the amount of play on both sides of the lanes that has touched off much controversy in bowling, especially in the ranks of the professionals. To keep the percentages in the proper perspective, there are about fifteen left-handers in every one hundred pro bowlers, slightly above the national average. There seems to be general agreement that this 15 percent of the bowlers is winning considerably more than 15 percent of the prize monies.

Why have left-handers been doing so well? The dressing is applied in heavier doses on the right side, that we are agreed on; and a rule of thumb is that it's applied once a day. But, once the day's bowling action has started—let's say it is league action—all those balls rolling over and through the oil will start pushing it aside and even making some of it vanish. The oil begins to break down (lose its consistency) on the right side. There are some who will flatly state that the oil breaks down quicker than it did years ago because the new synthetics being used do not have the durable properties they once did. There may be some substance to that school of thought.

At any rate, over on the other side of the lane, in a league that conforms to the national ratio of one left-hander to every ten bowlers, the oil that has been applied is not getting very much play on it. Certainly it is not undergoing the workout the right side is receiving. The logical consequence then is that the left-hander, once he's "found his line" to the pocket, can keep right on playing that line and make little or no adjustment. Left-handers often are rolling on a surface that is smooth, while the right-hander is constantly floundering.

Bowlers who have not reached the point of sophistication where they can detect the shifting of oil on the right side suffer most. It shows up in their scores as the evening or league session progresses. They start out playing one line and find they're doing rather well. But as the session wears on the oil may shift or break down, and the line they had been playing, the track they thought they'd found, suddenly isn't there anymore. They don't know how to adjust their line, or they make improper adjustments and pay the price in lower scores. The left-hander, however, hasn't had to contend with oil giving way over what may have been a wide track at best. That shot he has started out with, the one over the second arrow, will continue to serve him well right through the final frame of his final game.

My advice is elementary in the case of the right-hander who finds that the oil has shifted or evaporated and that his ball now has started to hook much more as it goes over a drier surface. You'll just have to make an instant reckoning when you see it happening and change your line, using the parallel line system. If you're perfectly coordinated in your footwork and arm swing, you'll need only one shot to zero in on a new line.

It's hard for the bowler to comprehend why he has to make such radical adjustments in his game because of the vagaries of the dressing used on the lanes. And he's often disturbed because he feels that perhaps his talent may be greater than someone else's but he has to pay the price the condition exacts. Many a locker room argument has been fomented by the lefty-righty syndrome in bowling, especially in professional bowling, where every little movement has a meaning of its own. For some time now various solutions have been sought in an effort to equalize conditions on both sides of the lanes. It is to be assumed, however, that the situation never will be fully resolved. Every time a left-hander won a tournament, there'd no doubt be speculation that he won because he had things his way; and were the winner a right-hander, it seems only reasonable to assume the left-hander would be convinced that conditions were altered to favor the righty. If you want to learn how controversial bowling is, just ask any of the forty million bowlers who have learned enough about the game to know that the oil on the lanes will determine to some extent how well he does.

The proprietor, remember, aside from knowing that the dressing will affect the game of bowlers, goes through this daily process mostly because he wants to preserve the life of his lane. A properly dressed lane will last about twenty years, but only about half that time if he is derelict in maintenance. However, even after ten or twenty years of use, the lane is not ready for the fireplace.

The proprietor can call in the people who installed his lanes, or a service organization, and have the lanes turned. That is actually the process involved—turning the lanes. The entire wooden bed is uprooted and turned over. The wood on the bottom side is the same as the wood on the top, only it is smooth-surfaced and hasn't undergone the rigors of thousands upon thousands of games over a score of years. Experts sand the lanes and apply lacquer and dressing and the lanes are good for another ten or twenty years of uninterrupted bowling—and controversy.

The resurfacing of lanes is vital, of course, and even here the equipment is varied and specialized. There are machines that scrape down the wood lengthwise and machines that do the job from side to side. It's just about the same process as that used to apply dressing. There are also machines that are used to detect high boards on a lane—boards that may have loosened and are protruding from the lane. These machines will locate the errant board and then a decision must be made as to whether the board can be put in its proper place or must be replaced. Should the latter be necessary, the board or boards are chipped out or taken out with a rotary blade. It is possible, too, that touch-up work with a mallet or sandpaper will get the job done without too much fuss.

Though nails and screws are used on the lanes, these never are evident. The holes made by them are covered with dowels and the final joining process is with cement or a heavy-duty glue. The laying of an alley bed is quite a refined process and if you are ever privileged to see one being installed, or being turned, you'll find it most interesting.

The resurfacing of alleys is not confined to just the lane itself. The channels and approaches are also done and the approaches require as much attention as the lanes, for it's here that the game begins. Just as is done on the lane, the approach has its old finish removed. Any one of many available approach finishes then is applied, restoring the approach to its original look. The bowler will often find after the approach is resurfaced and refinished that it is sticky. This may necessitate the use of a large steel wool pad on the approach for the first week or so until the surface is smooth once again. Naturally, humidity plays a key role in how you will or won't slide, but it usually comes right down to maintenance. Constant and diligent maintenance on every part of the lane, channels, and approach will pay off in the long run to the proprietor in money saved and bowlers retained.

Until you fully understand what goes on the lane, as well as what goes into your game, you'll remain a mediocre bowler. The bowler who goes on to bigger and better scores knows every facet of the game and knows it well. And when there's an innovation or a refinement made in some aspect of his game, he's right there to be an observer or an interrogator.

6.

The Ball

IT is virtually impossible to get a true count on how many different bowling balls are manufactured. While the basic properties of the ball are rubber and plastic and cork, there is much more to the sphere than its consistency. The location of the finger holes, the number of finger holes, and how the ball itself is drilled insofar as distribution of weight is concerned all play a role.

You'll hear one group of bowlers sing the praises of this ball, and another denounce that same ball as worthless. You'll hear some bowlers say you can't get a true roll, or grab the lane properly with a plastic ball and you'll hear another contingent claim that plastic gets the job done much better than rubber and is more pleasing to the eye, for only the plastic balls come in such a variety of colors.

The better the bowler, the more committed he is to the merits of one ball as opposed to another. Of course, many bowlers are on the staffs of ball manufacturers so it goes without saying that they will not go without saying *their* ball is best. If there really was one that did it all for all bowlers, there'd be no competition among the manufacturers. What makes it so interesting and intriguing is that certain kinds of bowling balls can do different things for different bowlers.

Bowlers usually stress how they have their balls drilled, where the finger holes are located, how the weight is distributed. Those are real factors, something we can deal with rationally. So, let's discuss bowling balls with an eye toward what they do for you and what you can do with them.

All rubber bowling balls have a hard core inside and then there are layers of rubber and cork before the shell of hard rubber is applied. The outside is then sanded down so we get the smooth surface we must have and then a heavy-duty wax is applied to give the ball a protective finish. When you purchase a hard rubber ball, that's all you see: a smooth, shiny black surface with the manufacturer's name on it.

In the beginning, bowling balls were made of wood and had only a thumbhole; you palmed the release. Then, bowling balls were made of rubber and had only two holes drilled into them. It was as simple as that: one hole for the thumb and one for the middle finger. No one asked why, no one knew that possibly it should be done in a different manner. That was the fashion and that's the way it was. Then someone recognized that a lot of pressure was being put on only two fingers. Why not put one more hole in the ball? It would be much easier on the hand. Enter: the three-finger bowling ball and that's the way it is right now and that's the way it figures to stay for some time.

People who suffer from arthritis or similar ailments, or people who possibly have lost fingers in accidents quite often have extra finger holes put in their balls. It was probably that way, too, in the day of the two-finger ball—someone inserting an extra hole to relieve a physical situation. A person who wants to go bowling and who does not have the power in his fingers to hold and toss the ball with the prescribed fingers should (and can) have an extra finger hole or two added.

High-averaged bowlers have invoked the privilege of being able to drill holes in their ball to accomplish something else. Many of them will drill a hole they never intend sticking a finger into for the sole purpose of adding weight to another part of the ball. Each time you drill a hole, you are taking away just so much weight from one side and actually "adding" it to the other. To preclude bowling balls that look like Swiss cheese, the Professional Bowlers Association allows its members only one extra "weight hole" in addition to the actual finger holes. This shifting of weights in a ball can be done by the pro from tournament to tournament depending on the condition of the lanes and what he wants his ball to do.

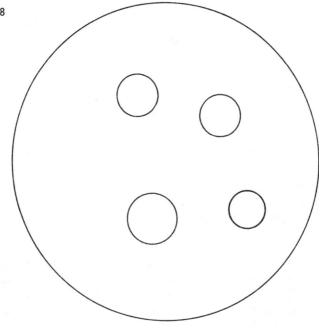

The smaller hole to the right is not simply another finger hole. The better bowler, seeking a weight distribution that will help his shot at a particular bowling center, will take out some weight from the "weight block," which will make his ball react in a specific manner

At least two professional bowlers I know often use a ball that has not two, but actually one wide hole, called a "slot," to accommodate two fingers. There is absolutely no bridge between the fingers. The bowlers who use the slot ball feel they get a more comfortable grip that way and as an offshoot of that comfort get a uniform lift as they come out of the ball on release.

I have experimented on several occasions with just such a ball, but I didn't have too much success with it. That's not to say that it won't help some bowlers. I'm sure if such fellows as Don Johnson and Mike Durbin use the slot, or have used it, they must know what they're doing. But I don't recommend

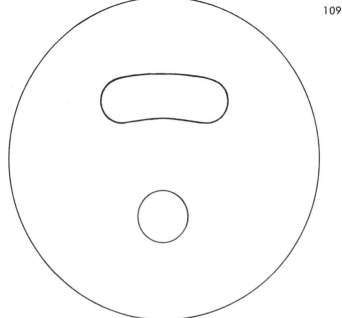

This is a "slotted" ball. Instead of two finger holes to accommodate the middle and ring fingers, the holes are joined and both fingers are actually in the same hole

that the middle average or newcomer fool around with this kind of ball, at least not on his own. If you are having a problem with your game, first visit your local pro or drop around to the pro shop. The pro probably will be able to analyze your game much better than you can. If he thinks the slotted ball will help, then give it a try. Don't prescribe for yourself unless you reach the status of high-averaged bowler or are a professional.

In the beginning of your bowling career, your only decisions must be as to color and weight, the latter on the advice of someone who perhaps knows your game better than you do. Take your ball to a qualified pro, one who is also an experi-

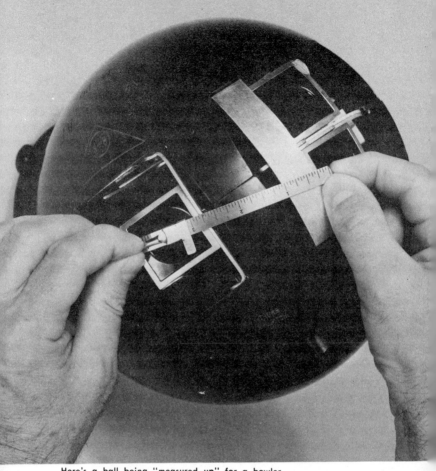

Here's a ball being "measured up" for a bowler

enced ball-driller; he will measure you with the particular kind of ball-fitting machine he uses. A popular machine is the one that looks like a replica of a regulation size bowling ball, except that it has many, many holes in it and also a sort of swivel center to allow him to measure not only the size of your fingers but the span of your hand as well.

Actually, the width of the finger is measured first by means of a removable slot that is placed in the proper hole after it is found to conform to the finger. When all three finger sizes are determined, the blocks in place, the bowler then inserts thumb first, middle and ring fingers next. Now the driller-pro has to measure the span. If the ball is to have a conventional grip, the fingers will be inserted up to the second joint. If it's to be a fingertip grip, the fingers will go in only as far as the first joint.

Many bowlers have the misconception that a fingertip grip means only that the finger holes are not drilled as deep as they are with a conventional grip. Wrong. Fingertip grips are determined solely by how wide the span of the ball is made. If the span is made longer, it's a fingertip; shorter and it's a conventional grip. With all that information jotted down on a card, the driller can go to work. But don't forget that this is ball-drilling in its simplest form. No allowances for weight distribution or "pitch" (direction in which the finger holes go) have been made. That's big-league talk and reserved for the bowler who feels he's equipped to make his ball do different things in different situations.

I don't want to go too deeply into the pitch of your ball, because any counseling you receive should come from your own ball specialist. But to help you know what it's all about, and to round out your bowling vocabulary, let me tell you a few things about pitch and the variables.

In most instances, bowlers will get too involved with the slant of their finger holes. They'll ask for thumb and finger holes that are conventional, meaning that the direction the holes take is right toward the center of the ball. But, as you know, if you take in the action going on to your right and left any time you go bowling, not everyone is built the same. A ball that is perfect for you might ruin another's game.

It is possible that the structure of your hand may dictate that the holes in your ball take an unconventional route. Perhaps the driller may recommend side pitch. In this process, the holes are slanted toward the palm of your hand. As a matter of fact, this is sometimes referred to as "palm pitch," for it means that fingers actually are heading toward the thumb when you put all three digits in the ball.

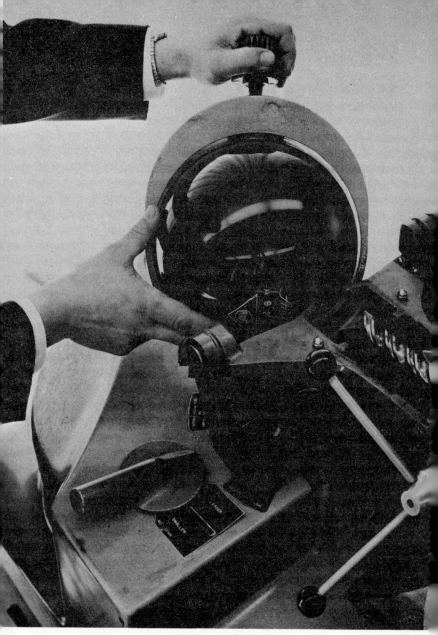

Two views of the ball-drilling apparatus

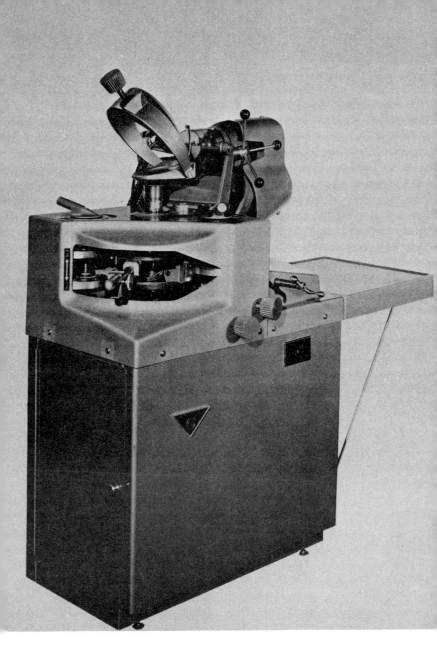

It may be that the man who is working out the details of your bowling ball will recommend back pitch. In this one, the slant is such that the thumb and other two fingers are taking a route away from center, away from each other.

To name but a few other variations in grip, more by way of indicating how involved it can get, let me tell you about something called the Ned Day Grip, named for a one-time outstanding bowler. This one calls for increased distance between the thumb and ring finger, purportedly to give the bowler a more powerful lift. What they also do here is pitch the two fingers toward the palm, while leaving the thumbhole conventional.

There are schools of thought on the various grips which almost defy belief. You'll find one bowler with the thumbhole offset to the left or right, and another who has one finger hole considerably higher or lower than the other. When you get so good at the game that you know why you're doing something, that's the time for you to try all those things.

Only in the last three or four years have bowlers come to realize that the bowling ball was designed to allow them to do things to it to make for different actions.

It may have taken the bowler a long time to become aware of these refinements available to him, but once he got the message, he really moved into high gear. The Professional Bowlers Association has done much to turn theory into science through experimentation by its members. Pro bowlers have learned that by shifting weights in different positions on the ball you will get different reactions.

There are finger weight, thumb weight, right-side weight, and left-side weight. To give you a picture of just what we are about to get into, hold your hand out in front of you, palm up, thumb drawn toward the center of your hand. That's about the way you will be holding your hand in the set position and on release. If you have just straight finger weight in your ball —nothing else—you'll find that the ball will skid much farther down the lane before breaking toward the pocket. A bowler who wants a ball that has a sharper bend near the end, one that will dive into the pocket, wants this kind of weight in his ball under certain conditions.

Thumb weight will make for a reaction that is the reverse of finger weight. Straight thumb weight will get the ball into its hooking "orbit" much sooner and then make it taper off somewhere as it nears the pocket. The pros call this "settling" action. I might very easily go for a ball with straight thumb weight if the lanes are hooking very much, and I want to make sure that I don't hook the ball too much and come in too heavily on the headpin.

Right-side weight will help the ball go into a movement where it will careen toward the pocket. If you see signs that indicate you may have a problem getting the ball to go on a true course toward the 1-3, putting right-side weight into your ball may turn the trick.

In keeping with the reasoning behind applying right-side weight to give the ball a better chance at getting up to the pocket, ask your pro to give you left-side weight if you are try- ing to accomplish something else. Application of weight to the left side will serve to hold the ball back somewhat and take away some of the overdrive toward the pocket you may have been getting.

Bowlers who are trying to get their ball to do more than one specific thing may go in for a selection of the above-listed weighting. One bowler, for example, may have finger weight *and* right-side weight. His intention is to have the ball he throws delay going into its hooking action and then have it blast into the key spot at the right time. You can readily see how toying with the various weighting methods available can be rather tricky. It's definitely not for novices—only for the veteran bowler who knows full well what he's doing and is entitled to toy with his game. Let your pro shop operator be your guide.

Let me illustrate how the pro's mind works under certain con- ditions. Suppose I came into a house for a tournament and the lanes were extremely "tight," meaning it was tough to get the ball to hook. I'd want my ball to hold the line for a distance (finger weight) and then go into the hooking action needed to knock down pins. On the other hand, if the lanes were really hooking, my battle plan would change drastically. Now I would want to have a ball with thumb weight and left-side (opposite pocket) weight. These act as reins on my shot and keep me from getting it to the critical pocket area too soon.

It's elementary that with so many weight combinations available to the bowler, he might need a van to haul around all the bowling balls that could be drilled. If you decide you want—or need—more than one ball, make certain you get the kinds that will help your game. You'll impress no one if you have six or seven balls, though most pros use more than one.

As a professional bowler, most of my livelihood came from what I earned in competitive bowling and I'd have done myself a terrible disservice if I didn't experiment and do everything within my power to improve my game. In the past I have tried thumb weight, but it doesn't seem to help my game. On one of my bowling balls I have straight finger weight and on another I have finger weight plus right-side weight.

The dimensions may vary, but built into every bowling ball is a "weight block"

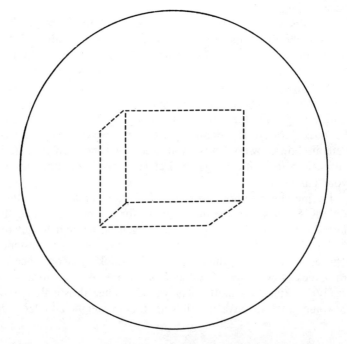

I've been talking at great length about ball-weighting. This does not mean that weight is applied to the ball. When I talk about weighting of the ball it means something is taken away from one area to make the ball heavier on the opposite side. It's time now to get into the intricacies of weight distribution, a new bowling science, because bowlers have been slow in coming to realize that it can help make or break their game.

Every manufacturer inserts—smack under the label—a weight block. This is the heaviest part of the ball and it's made of hard rubber in a rubber ball, and plastic in a plastic ball, though there may be an alloy in the plastic ball—rubber and plastic. The weight block, located just below the shell, can come in assorted shapes. It can be square or pancake style, and one manufacturer inserts his weight block in cylindrical form. The pertinent data is printed on the box in which the ball is shipped to the pro shop. It might say: sixteen pounds, three ounces, meaning the gross weight of the ball is sixteen pounds, with three of those ounces the weight block. It's the three ounces with which we can work. Some manufacturers will allow for as much as six ounces.

If we are dealing with a square, you can visualize what you would have to do to get the desired weights in certain parts of the ball. By removing a portion of the square, in essence we are adding to another sector. That's the basis of what is to follow.

Let us say that you want finger weight in the ball. You want the ball to be heavier in that portion where your fingers will go. What you would do is move your grip down—start from a point below dead center (which is always indicated on the ball, in the area of the label). By departing from dead center, you've allowed more weight to remain on the upper portion. You always move the grip in a direction opposite the one in which you want the ball to carry more weight.

Depending on the manufacturer, the weight block will be located from a quarter inch to one inch below the surface. The man who drills the ball out will know its location and shape.

Let's say you located dead center on the ball, went down a

quarter inch, and decided it was there that you wanted the thumbhole to be. By drilling the thumbhole in that location you would have given your ball about a half ounce of finger weight. That one example will serve as the basic rule to follow: If you want finger weight, you come down from dead center; if you want thumb weight, you go up from center; for right-side weight, move off the center spot to the left; and for left-side weight, go in the opposite direction.

This system of weight shifting should not even be considered by the bowler unless he's progressed to the 180 range or better. It's just too much for him to be involved with in the early stages of his game. Most pros who are schooled in shifting weights will be able to explain to the bowler what happens when certain things are done to the ball, but don't allow yourself to be talked into this phase unless you know that you are in the better-than-average category. However, once you've attained a measure of sophistication and ability, you'll find that it can work wonders with your game.

I'd say that about 85 percent of the ball drillers are thoroughly familiar with weight-shifting and about the same number of bowlers have come around to the system. It took some time before they learned what it could do for their game and more and more are now joining the ranks.

The two bowling balls I carry around are quite different. One has a half-ounce finger weight and a quarter-ounce right-side weight. The other has just a half-ounce finger weight. Each does a different job for me, depending on the lane condition I'm confronted with. To review: I use the finger-right-side weight ball when I want to get more hook; the straight finger-weight ball will skid more and then will begin a gradual end-over-end motion toward the pocket.

Here's something else you should bear in mind. It may take you three or four balls before you get the combination that is correct for you. There are so many forces at work in your game that you can't expect to hit the right combination first crack out of the box. There is no one who can just look at you, or your game, and be so arbitrary as to say, "Well, you need a half ounce here, and a quarter ounce there."

I mentioned earlier that professional bowlers are allowed one extra hole in their ball. To be sure, many pros use this privilege to make for even greater weight distribution or shifting. A hole drilled apart from the finger holes will add weight to the opposite side. A bowler may use that ball in one tournament and then, when he gets to the next site and sees that the condition requires a different kind of ball, he'll have that hole plugged up, a process every driller engages in. He merely pours rubber in its liquid state into the hole, allows it to dry and harden, and then smooths the surface.

When you finally have the kind of ball you want, and the one that will topple the most pins for you, it's time for an explanation of just what kind of ball you will throw. Bowlers have a name for each type of ball, because each one has a different look.

The full roller: the "track" will be located between the finger and thumbholes

The *full roller* is a ball that rolls toward the pins in an orbit between the thumb and finger holes. When the ball returns from the pit end, you can look at it and see a clearly defined line circling the ball right there. This kind of roll does not get as much hook on it—does not have that much hooking power—because it takes longer to get to the pocket, rolling as it does over its entire circumference.

The *semiroller* will show up as having been rolled outside the thumbhole, perhaps an inch or more farther down from the full roller. It will use up only about three quarters of the ball's circumference, where the full roller used all of the ball.

Then there's the *spinner,* which uses up only about one third of the ball, and here the line will be even lower than the semiroller's. Incidentally, the line we are speaking of is caused by dust and residue on the lanes, combined with the lane dressing.

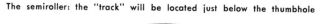

The semiroller: the "track" will be located just below the thumbhole

The revolution you put on the ball is determined by the position of the hand on release. To get the spinner going simply turn the wrist, with little or no lift on the ball. To get the semi-roller going you need a little of each, a turn of the wrist and a pronounced lift. The full roller is achieved by locking in the wrist, with the thumb in a nine o'clock position. When the thumb comes out, you're not lifting to the side, but actually lifting into the ball.

Is one kind of ball preferable to another? Well, I'd have to say—and almost all bowlers will agree—that the spinner is the *least* desirable. It's just not too energetic a ball. There was a time when all bowlers tried to achieve the full roller in the belief that it got more pins—which may have been so. As a matter of fact, many of these older bowlers still toss that kind of ball and refuse to waver. Today's lane conditions, however,

The "spinner": note that the track is located in a small area well below the thumbhole

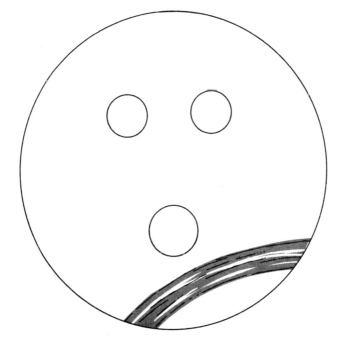

make the semi- or three-quarter roller the best to toss. That's the one that rolls just outside the thumbhole.

Most professional bowlers are using the semiroller and I guess you can't find too much fault with the brand of bowling we're getting these days. Scores are better than ever and to me that means that bowlers are better than ever, regardless of what anyone has to say about today's conditions.

There are only a handful of touring pros who use the full roller. They have their reasons and, if it works for them, they should by all means continue using that kind of ball. Even with the variance in lane conditions on the right and left sides, whether the bowler was righty or lefty would have little bearing on the situation. At least one of the handful I speak of who toss the full roller is a southpaw.

The kind of ball you select, the way the finger holes are drilled, how the weight is distributed, the weight of the ball itself, and the kinds of revolutions on the ball are all factors in how poorly or how well you bowl, or will bowl. Don't dismiss the importance of any, for all are interrelated. Now here are a few closing notes about the ball and the finger holes:

When the pro drills your ball, he will use a machine that routs out a round hole. That's the way the bit on the machine does its job. None of us, however, have perfectly round thumbs or fingers. The feel isn't always the best. I speak for myself and many other pros when I go into this next revelation. Many of us will take a sharp instrument and groove the sides of the holes so that they are somewhat egg-shaped.

None of us has a finger that is as big from front to back as it is from side to side, so why should the hole be symmetrical? When you have advanced to the next plateau in bowling, you will do well to pay heed to what I've just said. Get those holes so that your fingers feel snug and form-fitting.

Here's another trick many pros use to make sure they get a more comfortable grip on the ball. It could be used after a long layoff, or even a brief one. It's a method employed to compensate for a thumb that swells when you've bowled many games, and recedes when you've been inactive.

Let's say you haven't bowled for a week. You'll probably find that the thumbhole that was tailor-made for you feels too big. Take a few pieces of any tape that is smooth on one side —electrical tape will do the trick. Insert several strips of this tape into the thumbhole. As you bowl your finger will swell a bit, and as it does you can keep removing a layer of tape. You'll find, I believe, that when you've removed that last strip, your thumb will now fit perfectly into the hole.

Bowlers will insert strips of tape in the thumbhole and as their finger swells will remove the strips one by one

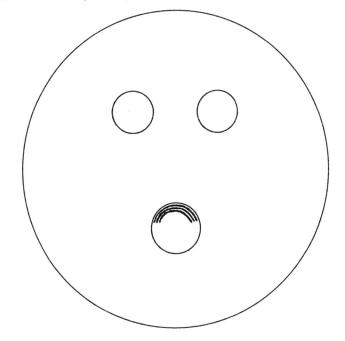

7.

Bowling Aids, Devices, and Gimmicks

THE game of bowling can be as simple or as complicated as you want it to be. If you want bowling to provide merely a form of exercise, which it does so well, there really is no need to get so deeply into the game that it requires more hours than you have to spare. Keeping bowling in the proper perspective will heighten your interest, improve your game, or provide therapeutic help—all three, or whichever you want.

People who are connected with the game—manufacturers, suppliers, proprietors—want the bowler to be happy. And they want his game to get better, if that's what he wants. Therefore a spate of bowlers' aids have been marketed almost since the game began. Old-timers will say that they needed nothing but a towel to keep their hands dry, but times have changed. Today's bowler has so many aids available that the choice can be difficult or beneficial or easy or worthless.

To know what is available and what each device is designed to do, here are some that are on the market—first those that have a specific purpose, and then some that have come and gone, leaving little impact on the bowling population.

Gloves

One of the most popular gloves is the Don Carter, which was made expressly for Don some years ago and since has been produced and sold by the millions. Its purpose is to take up the slack—the space—created when the fingers grip the ball.

The glove fits snugly over the fingers and has a padded center that brings your palm in contact with the ball, making for a comfortable grip. The cushion distributes the weight and feel of the ball over the entire hand and is designed to lessen the strain that may come with many games of bowling.

The Don Carter Glove, and its built-up palm, reduces pressure on the bowler's thumb and the intent is to eliminate or inhibit sore thumbs through reducing lateral pressure.

Of course, I like to think that the Lift-Tru, which carries my name, is among the most beneficial in that it enables the bowler to keep the wrist straight and do just what the name says—get a true lift on each shot. A piece of light-weight metal is inserted in the leather and will prevent the wrist from breaking. It is easy to put on.

There are various other gloves on the market, and one of

The Don Carter Glove

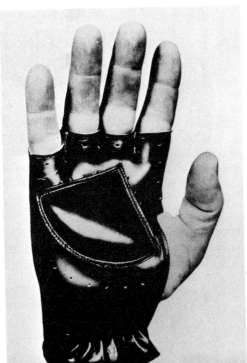

the newest to be adopted by a number of the pros is the
Don Johnson Gold Palm. This also slips over the fingers of
the bowling hand, but instead of a cushion built into the glove,
it has a plastic horseshoe which adheres to the glove. Unlike
the Don Carter Glove, the Gold Palm is adjustable, so that
a bowler who feels he is not coming out of the ball properly,
or who finds that he is not getting consistent control of the ball
may change the positioning at will.

Another device in the glove family, one that is also worn by
quite a few of the pros, is the Dick Weber Wrist-Master. As

The Don Johnson Gold Palm

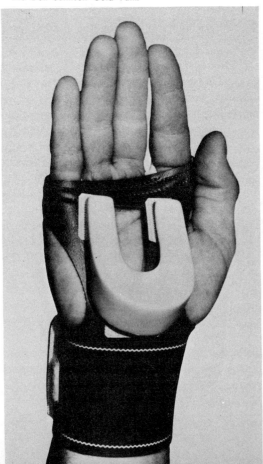

The Billy Welu Lift-Tru

with all other aids worn on the hand, its purpose is to eliminate wrist fatigue, ensure correct release, and keep the wrist straight, a problem with many bowlers. The Wrist-Master has helped Dick quite a bit. It maintains the wrist in the proper position through the entire delivery. A metal insert in the leather guarantees a stiff wrist. If your problem has been breaking the wrist as you come into the shot, this could be of great benefit.

Constructed along the same lines, but with a stiff leather substituted for the metal backing, is the Ace Mitchell Wrist Band. This has a thong that stretches across the heel of the palm, with the larger portion going on the wrist. The wording on the Wrist Band claims it will make for a better follow-through, and for many bowlers it probably does.

The names of these products are given and their benefits discussed so that the bowler will be aware of their availability. I am giving no endorsement to any in this book, but I do state that none will hurt your game. If you lean toward a corrective device, by all means try one or two or as many as you care to try. If the pros use them, you can be sure they will not be a detriment to their game. No pro is going to go so far overboard on a device as to jeopardize his livelihood.

Other Aids

Bowling has become so scientific in recent years that it is no longer sufficient for instructors to teach only the rudiments of good bowling and let it go at that. Weight distribution is discussed and often stressed and one school of thought has given rise to still another device.

One man—I believe he came from Fort Worth, Texas— stated that a bowler who was lifting a sixteen-pound bowling ball had to counterbalance that weight in some fashion so he'd be able to get up to the line on an even keel. There is some merit to what he has to say and I know several fellows who tried a corrective device. Some say it helped. What it amounted to was a one-pound weight sewn into a glovelike strap. I've seen many bowlers who still use it, and since they are, you can be sure it is helping them.

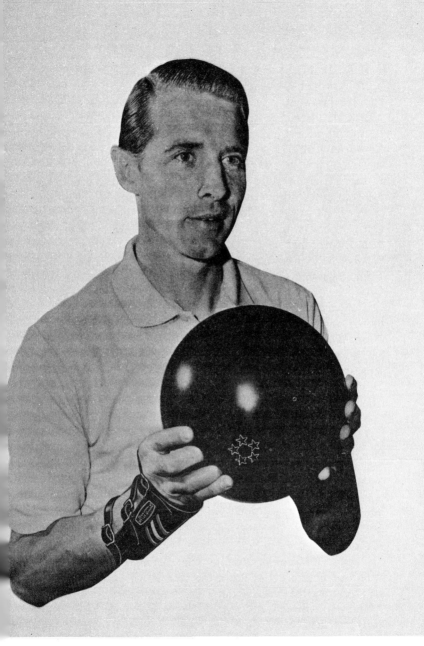
The Dick Weber Wrist-Master

Billy Hardwick, one of the best bowlers ever, used to have a problem with a flying elbow; he wasn't keeping it tucked in close to his waist when he went bowling. So some ingenious gent came up with a strap designed to correct that basic fault. Billy tried it for a few tournaments, I believe, but I don't think he—or any other bowler—uses it now. The strap was tied to the bowler's waist and then hooked up somewhere to his arm. It kept his elbow close in. Maybe the trouble was that it was too restrictive. Corrective devices and gimmicks are okay only if they don't go off the deep end. I certainly don't want to suggest to a bowler that he try a device to improve his game and then discover that the corrective measure led to a problem. The best bowler is a bowler who is thinking and swinging easy-like.

Some gimmicks have been ridiculous in design and purpose. One such, marketed some years ago, had no purpose that was apparent to me. It was a form of grip that attached to the ball with two suction cups. When you went through your down- and backswing it stayed in place, but on the release you had to sort of snap your arm or wrist and the handle then separated from the ball.

My advice is to keep away from anything that purports to change the game itself. Bowling offers more than enough to you and for you so you don't need any way-out gimmicks.

The bowler always has to have the proper feel of the ball and be perfectly comfortable with the one he is using. The slightest hesitancy in delivery or unsureness during any part of the approach or delivery will be ruinous. It is toward that end that many items are offered to guarantee a good grip. There are thumbhole and finger hole inserts, made of cork, rubber, and sandpaper. They have one specific aim: to give you a tighter grip on the ball.

Quite a few bowlers use leather coverings on either their thumb or fingers to cut down the chances of growing calluses or of cutting the hand. I don't use them, nor do I have any sentiments on such devices. If you're convinced they help, then give them a try.

In the heat of battle, or the heat of the day or night, the hand is liable to perspire, and precautions must be taken to keep the ball from slipping out of your hand. Practically all bowling centers have a hand dryer (fan) built into the ball return unit so that you can have your hand blown dry between shots. Some bowlers, however, have other means.

You can use a rosin bag to keep the hand dry. Almost all bowlers carry a hand towel. To show you how far that can go, many of the pros I know use a moist towel. The wetness of the towel wipes away the perspiration and then they use the hand dryer or rosin.

Some bowlers are never troubled with sore thumbs or fingers, while others are plagued with chronic tenderness or worse. You'll see liquid court plaster, clear plastic, and what have you. If they keep the fingers from cuts or bruises or calluses they're ideal. If you're thinking of using them because you see better bowlers using them, don't. The time to turn to medications is when something has gone wrong, or you have good reason to expect that it may.

The bowler who is troubled by something but does nothing about it is being more derelict than the bowler who dreams up ailments and defects. Prevention is much more advisable than cure in the case of bowling, but don't go about trying to prevent something that doesn't exist.

For each of the devices and gimmicks and artifices that I have touched on there probably are ten more in the same family. If any of them work for you, use them. If you don't need any, fine.

8.

The Psychology
of Bowling Well

ATTAINING a pinnacle in what you do, especially if what you do puts you in the public eye, is rarely accidental. Maybe there are different rules involved when you are engaged in a team sport, like baseball and football and basketball; you are always around guys whose sole purpose, presumably, is to see the team win, without regard to personal achievement. But in bowling, as in golf, quite often you are in the center of the stage all by yourself. At least that's the way it is in the professional ranks. It's not always sufficient just to have the natural ability, the instinct, and the drive. You must psych yourself up almost all the time before you go out and perform. No matter at what level you are at in bowling, your mental attitude, almost as much as your instinctive or acquired talents, will have a telling effect.

I don't believe a bowler—or any athlete—can do justice to himself or his game unless he adopts a psychology he wants to follow and makes a point of following. Before a bowler takes to the lanes he should draw up a mental picture of what he's doing, of what he wants to do, of the little keys to his game that he wants to remember. A bowler must be able to take thoughts from his subconscious into his conscious mind. I'm a firm believer in that. You must have a psychology of bowling before you can be a fine bowler.

I guess most bowlers psych themselves up in some fashion. I did it most of the times in my motel room before going to the lanes. Maybe I'll be lying in bed and it'll be nice and quiet and I'll get to thinking about what lies ahead for me at the lanes. That's the time to relax and analyze any problems I may have had in an earlier round of bowling and decide how to overcome them. It could be that I'll be involved in some major tournament and I'll try and draw a mental battle plan on what lines I'll be playing. I don't think the locker room, or any place where it's liable to be noisy, is the place to plan strategy. If you are to be able to concentrate on what you hope to achieve, you must have solitude; you should not be in surroundings where there is talk and people are milling around.

Some bowlers simply do not know how to give vent to their emotions when they are out on the lanes. You're all alone out there in pro competition and there's seldom anyone to tell your troubles to. Lacking a human sounding board, a bowler will often take out his anger or displeasure at some circumstance on something inanimate. He may kick an imaginary brick, or a very real ball return. He may mutter to some unseen person words he would never say to his face. Too often a terrible temper will be the undoing of a bowler. The game demands too much concentration to allow for tantrums. Almost all bowlers can point to some other bowler and flatly state something that goes like this: "He could be a much better bowler—almost unbeatable—if only he'd learn to curb his temper."

You've heard it, I've heard it, and all of us have said similar words on many an occasion. There is one bowler I know of who has a wicked temper. It was even worse in years gone by and he tried many methods of curbing his anger when things did not always go the way he would have liked. A friend of his, a psychologist, cut a record for him and he took it on tour with him. In his motel room he'd play the record on which the doctor had spoken soothing and reassuring words. The process here was reversed. Here the words were passing through the conscious mind into the subconscious in the hopes that they would become imbedded forever.

It was almost like hypnosis, if indeed it wasn't just that. The doctor friend hoped that the words he spoke to his hothead friend would go so deep within him that he'd never have to stop and recall how he was supposed to suppress his ire in any given situation. I don't believe he uses the record any longer, but he did listen to it for a long period of time and I think it helped him, even though he is still given to bursts of temper once in a while.

I have never gone in for any such assistance, but what I do is a form of self-hypnosis. I think of my "game plan" over and over. I once listened to the record I spoke about above, so I know just what the message on it was. What does the trick is the repetition involved. Any time you read something or hear something over and over, some of what you read or hear has to rub off and do some good. After a time, what you have forced yourself to do becomes so natural you don't need prodding in any form.

The reputation I have is of being a very even-tempered person. It may appear that way, but you can't suppress your feelings all the time. You must have an outlet, you must let go frequently. Maybe the secret is resolving to yourself just which way you're going to show anger or frustration or what have you. And where you do it is important, too, if you are to retain your image before the public.

There is absolutely no connection between performance and temperament. You can give vent to your anger and it need not affect your play. Only when you keep it stored up inside can it destroy you and your game, or when you do something rash that can turn the public against you and even *you* against you.

Ted Williams, one of baseball's all-time great players, had a notorious reputation for losing his temper. But he used fits of anger to good advantage. Maybe he played his best games when he got the juices flowing. I'm not going to take a stand and say you're better off being placid, as opposed to letting yourself go.

It could depend on your upbringing, just what makes you angry and the methods you have in psyching yourself. Some bowlers—as well as athletes in other sports—deliberately prod themselves to a point of anger as a means of firing themselves up for an important match or game. If it gets the adrenalin going, all well and good.

It may just be that you require more than soothing words to quell your anger. What can you do to allow some of that venom to escape? If your game is suffering because you're never able to blow off steam, here are some ideas that may help:

One pro bowler—and a very good one—comes on the lanes with a handful of pencils and when things go wrong, or he suspects they might be going wrong, he reaches into his back pocket, grabs a pencil, and snaps it in two—or four, if it's a long pencil.

A lot of fellows I've crossed lanes with through the years actually curse on the lanes, but no one ever hears the words. They've conditioned themselves to a sort of quiet release of steam, so the words are spoken, but are inaudible to others.

One of the favorite tricks of better bowlers—better hot-tempered ones, that is—is to "run out their strikes." What they do when they see the ball heading on a true line for the pocket is a sort of shuffle to the left or right as ball hits pins. In this manner, if all ten pins didn't fall down, at least some of that pent-up emotion will have been dissipated.

One of the best at "running them out" is Dave Davis and you'll sometimes see him wind up four or five lanes away after his ball made contact. Don't try this maneuver in regular league play too often, for you may just start bumping into people! The pros can get away with it because their "courtesy code" prohibits bowlers a few lanes to the left and right from stepping up on the approach when another bowler is there.

Other tension relievers or temper soothers? Raise your hands upward in dismay, or look downward in disgust. Pound your fist (lightly) into your palm or hitch up your trousers or grind your teeth. All the guys do.

Golf and bowling have a number of revealing similarities. While the bowler is lost—or should be—in thoughts about what boards and angles to play, the golfer is primarily concerned with wind velocity and depth of sand or grass. The equipment may differ, and the playing areas may be worlds apart, but the psychologies involved in both games are very much the same.

I've been asked by many younger bowlers for advice on how to control their tempers out on the lane. There's no simple, single answer; it's more of a long-range project. I'd tell them to room with someone who has less of a trigger temper; that has to rub off. I know of one young bowler who is on the staff of the American Machine & Foundry Company, for whom I once did clinical and exhibition work. I have noticed a radical change in him and I hope it's because I've been influential with him. He no longer is as carefree when he's bowling as he once was and he's concentrating much more than he did. I keep coming back to that word—concentration—because I really believe it's the key to good performance. This fellow's bowling, always good, has got better and will continue to improve once he learns to channel all his thoughts properly.

A professional bowler has very little chance anymore to engage in team bowling. In the pro ranks, of course, it's all singles competition. There is a tremendous difference between the two. In team competition, the bowling is much slower, hence it is much easier to be distracted. The pro tour never allows more than two men on a lane and the result is faster bowling, more concentration, and the opportunity to groove in on your game faster and better.

It isn't easy to compete and be at your best unless someone is giving you an occasional pat on the back or you hear words of encouragement. There are times when the bowlers do this for each other, and even offer some brand of constructive criticism. It can be awfully lonely out there.

The format of all Professional Bowlers Association tournaments forces bowlers to change emotions in midstream. In the qualifying phase of play, there are four bowlers on a pair of lanes and each roots for the others to do their best and to keep going on to the finals. For the first couple of days, you're just going for high scores. Once the qualifying segment ends, the tournament turns into a man-against-man format. It's one against the other, the winner to receive a bonus for scoring a victory. It's at this point that you wish the other fellow good luck, and then go out and try to beat him. There is an interesting psychology to this part of the tournament and you can't be anything but good-natured about it. If you beat a guy, he might just turn around the next time you're up against him and whip you. It's better, in the long run, to keep the competition on a friendly basis.

Bowling has many advantages over a team sport. The accent is on individual performance, and you have to shift for yourself. You have the opportunity of picking your own friends. You make up your own mind as to who you want to travel with and how you want to travel. It makes everything out on the tour much easier.

All of us have some quirk, some idiosyncracy as we go into our delivery. For some it may be too quick a first step, or too slow a second or third step. Maybe you have a hitch in your swing, or you sometimes forget to face your target area squarely. Golfers have the answer, and don't forget how similar bowling and golf are. The good golfer always pictures his shot before his swing. You do the very same thing.

Give yourself reminders such as, "I'm going to go up there completely relaxed, I'm going to have a smooth approach and a smooth delivery." Picture the shot and you'll heighten your chances of making it.

Too many bowlers play the game of second-guessing themselves when they're up on the approach. The time to prescribe treatment or to prod yourself into the right frame of mind is the settee area while you're waiting your turn to shoot.

If you've ever watched the television shows on Pro Bowlers Tour, where there are many thousands of dollars at stake, you'll notice how detached—how disinterested—the bowler waiting his turn seems to be. It appears that he couldn't care less just how the man at the line is doing. In some respects this is true. Naturally, there is an interest in how your opponent is faring, but that's secondary. You must be intent on planning your next shot, what angle you'll be playing, whether to move a board or two on the approach or out on the lane. You have too much to concentrate on to play the role of spectator when the man you're trying to beat is shooting.

If every part of you is working toward one goal—the strike, or the spare—the execution of that shot will not be nearly so difficult when it's your turn.

With every one of us constantly in pursuit of perfection in bowling, here's another point you should mark down and retain. It concerns the perfect game—the 300 all of us are seeking. It's also probably the only time you should ever become score-conscious.

The bowler who gets up in the last frame telling himself something like, "If I get a double it'll give me a 234 and high game for the night," is not going about bowling in the proper manner. Having a goal in sight will do much for you. If you know that a double will give your team a victory, even though it may only give you a game in the 150s, that's really the name of the game.

When you've a chance at a 300, that's something else. Those times I've gone for them have always been exciting. And then it's time to get nervous, but you must learn to control yourself; take a deep breath and exhale just before the shot. Once you get that first strike in the tenth frame you seem to be on your way; that's the tough one. But here too, mapping your strategy on the next shot will help more than saying, "Wow, just a couple more and I've got a 300."

Take a game where you need a strike in the last frame to lock the other fellow out of a chance for victory. The odds are you're not going up there with the thought in mind that a strike will give you such and such a score. You're strike-conscious only because it will sew up victory, and you should be playing the shot just as you did early in the game, when a strike was a strike, and not a game-clincher.

Good scoring will follow good thinking. It has to.

I have one final tip on the game's psychology I'd like to pass along. It works for me and it will for you.

Draw a picture in your mind of just how you look going up

to the line to release a ball. Visualize the rhythm involved, the number of steps you will take, any keys you can find in your approach. Then, take five minutes to relax completely. A great time would be just before you set out for the lanes and your night's bowling. When you get to the lanes, you'll feel almost as though you've been through it all and have it down pat. The only difference will be that there's no fatigue involved—just concentration. When your time comes to bowl, it'll seem much easier to do the right things. The fellow who comes abruptly from some other activity and immediately starts his game will hardly ever begin properly. That's when those 150 games pop up, when you know you really aren't that bad.

Stay in the right frame of mind and you'll have automatically developed a great psychology for bowling. Be moderate in your actions and reactions, learn the pleasures of being a good sport and a good loser, and try to control your temper so that it will not betray you in a game that requires as much of your mind at it does of your body.

Anyone can excel once in a while, but it's the champion who excels most of the time. Be loyal to yourself and to your fans and your good thinking will bear fruit in the form of superior bowling.

9.

So You Want to Be a Pro

EVERY word, every intimation, every suggestion that has preceded this section of the book has had two purposes: to make you enjoy bowling much more than you have, and to make you a better bowler. The two are interrelated, of course, especially if you want the game to propel you into something more significant than league bowling. If you bowl strictly as a means to unwind and to give yourself a feeling of accomplishment, all well and good. But there are many among you who will get so proficient at bowling that you won't be content merely to pass the time in open or league competition.

The Professional Bowlers Association, like other sports organizations, has given bowling a hierarchy, an elite corps. The bowlers who are included in the roster of the PBA are accepted as the world's best. Though the game may have started, as some historians say, in Egypt or Babylon or wherever, today it's an American game. True, the sport has spread to all corners of the world, but no one plays the game as the American does. Maybe someday someone somewhere will catch up, but right now the standard in bowling is the American competitor.

In years gone by, there were many directions the better bowler could go. There were the exhibitions and competitions engaged in by teams sponsored by beer and other affluent companies. I stress beer firms because there was an abundance of firms involved in the game. They paid salaries, entry fees, and travel expenses for fellows who became, in essence, their representatives. While beer and bowling still are helpmates to an extent, it is more on a provincial level these days.

The accent on touring teams has diminished, if not vanished. Bowling's upper echelon was organized in 1958, when an Akron, Ohio, attorney, Eddie Elias, gathered together thirty-three of the country's biggest name bowlers and formed the Professional Bowlers Association. From that year to the present, the image of the professional bowler has turned from team player to singles performer.

In 1959, the PBA conducted its first three tournaments, and the gross value of those events was $47,000. But the ground had been broken. There now was a pinnacle toward which every young bowler could aspire. In 1960 there were seven tournaments and prize monies totaled $150,000. Television shows on which PBA members competed began to go into production and no few of these were shown nationally and viewed by millions of fans. One year later the PBA offered to its ever-growing membership eleven tournaments and money that was now at the quarter-million-dollar mark. In was in this year, 1961, that the biggest step was taken in the acceleration of professional bowling's impact on the public. It was the telecast, on a nationwide scale, of the finals of a professional tournament. The site was Paramus, New Jersey, and the event was the National Invitational.

Since then, the PBA's growth has been phenomenal. Today, there are about thirty-five tournaments each year, and the money bowlers aim for totals of about two million dollars. In addition, several giants of business have become involved in the cosponsorship of tournaments proper, and/or in the cosponsorship of the television show that is now aired on a thirteen-week basis. Bowling has become big business, where once it was strictly good business.

Tournaments have been held outside the continental limits of the United States—in Hawaii, Venezuela, Japan, and Puerto Rico. Professional bowling has taken bowling's big names and made them even bigger. The stars of the game are recognized and idolized by millions of sports fans and they are pointed out on the street perhaps even more often than the luminaries of other sports because the people who see bowling events are in closer proximity to the bowler than, say, a professional football player whose identity is hidden by bulky and obscuring equipment.

The professional bowler who makes it big can *really* make it big. He will—or can—receive the opportunity to endorse products and places, to appear on television, and to make personal appearances for which he is remunerated, and, don't forget, has available to him prize monies from not only those events organized by the PBA, but in many others backed by bowling proprietors.

A young man who has the ability and character could do worse than aim for a career in professional bowling. Even the qualifications set a standard that is established in few other sports. Once you've made the grade—been accepted as a member of the Professional Bowlers Association—and vied with the best, there's a wonderful feeling of pride that envelops you. Let me set down here some of the requirements for joining:

(a) A minimum average of 190 for your most recent two years of competition. Applicants who cannot meet this requirement, but who feel there is an extenuating circumstance, may have their application reviewed by the PBA Tournament Committee, made up of PBA members.

(b) A fine reputation.

(c) Willingness to perform in at least one PBA-sponsored tournament per year.

(d) Willingness to serve a one-year apprenticeship before becoming a full-fledged member.

(e) Must be at least eighteen years of age.

Once those requirements are met, the applicant must have affixed to his application the signature of one of the PBA Regional Directors or Representative, or three PBA members in good standing in the region where the applicant resides.

Another requirement is that the local American Bowling Congress secretary provide all requested league information pertinent to you. Applicants must pay an initiation fee and thereafter an entry fee to perform in tournaments.

Upon his acceptance as a member, the bowler is eligible to compete for prize monies (if he is under nineteen, a letter of consent for him to bowl for prize money must accompany his application), is included in a group insurance plan, and may avail himself of the PBA's Job Placement Bureau.

Naturally, there may be ramifications to some of the above-listed requirements, but that's basically what it's all about when you decide to become a pro. Depending on how many competitions you decide to enter, how much money you win in any given year, and just where you do your bowling, you will fall into a definite classification.

There are categories known as Touring Professionals (Group I), Touring Professionals (Group II), Resident Professionals (Group I) and Resident Professionals (Group II). The Touring Professional (Group I) is the hard core of the PBA. It means that in the preceding calendar year he has competed in two-thirds of the cosponsored tournaments and/or was among the leading twenty-five money-winners on the official earnings list compiled by the PBA.

So much stress is placed on the caliber of the young men who join the organization that some years ago a group of pro bowlers were drawn from the membership to form an Image Committee. The purpose of this group, and it remains so today, was to establish a set of rules whereby the professional bowler might comport himself in a manner befitting his station in the sporting world.

A pamphlet is issued yearly, and revisions and additions are made periodically, so that the bowler may read the printed word and learn how to improve or enhance his image before the public and press. Such items as dress, behavior, courtesy, and cleanliness are touched upon and the bowler can even go one step farther as he strives to better himself and his game.

Not long ago a series of tapes was purchased by the PBA and given to the membership. They all deal with one subject—self-improvement. Step inside the locker room at any PBA tournament and you are liable to see a pro with tape recorder in hand and earplug in place listening to a tape that will tell him how to control his temper better in the face of a disappointing situation—or how to apply himself to the solution of a problem where the problem might have seemed insoluble.

The professional bowler is a breed unto himself and we like to think that all of us who are members, and who battle constantly to upgrade our game and ourselves, stand apart and possibly above any group similarly engaged in play for pay. There are about one thousand of us and the membership rolls keep growing, almost keeping pace with the growth of the tournaments and available monies and fame to be earned.

And now, just in case you are among those who possibly have never seen a professional bowling tournament—a tournament conducted by the Professional Bowlers Association— suppose I take you through a typical tournament and tell you exactly what happens. The format was carefully worked out and meticulously executed by a large staff connected with the PBA.

Though there might be some variation as to when they are held, generally all PBA events begin with a professional-amateur competition, a pro-am for short. For many weeks, even months prior to a tournament, bowlers may sign up to compete when the pros get to town. For a fixed sum, an average bowler —by average I mean a handicap league competitor—will gain entry into the pro-am. Many bowling centers conduct a novel series of mini-tournaments so that the lucky or high-scoring amateurs may win spots without paying the fixed stipend.

When the pros arrive, pairings are made and generally it works like this:

Each pro will be assigned to a pair of lanes and his "partners" in that one game will be several amateurs. While only the pro's actual game score counts, each amateur is given a handicap, much in the same fashion as he is when he bowls in his league. After each game, the amateur's gross score (actual game plus handicap) is added to the score recorded by the pro. Let's say the amateur rolled a 165 game, and had a 35-

pin handicap. That means he "shot" a 200. If the pro rolled a 235 game, that amateur's one-game total would be 435. Now, the pro moves on to another set of amateurs and another pro moves into the picture. The same format will hold true for him, and then still a third pro.

All pro-ams are three games long and at the end of the session the amateur whose total pinfall, combined with his three pros' pinfalls, is the highest is the winner of first-prize money from a prize fund that has been established by the management, depending on the number of entrants who are competing. Naturally there are lesser prizes paid out.

There are quite a few deviations from this format, and one of them may be an incentive plan worked out by the host proprietor. He may offer merchandise or vacations—any variety of things—to his amateur entrants to get them to join in the fun. The formula has been successful and it is self-perpetuating.

Since people are star-conscious—and rightfully so—where it is practical, only the more famous pros are assigned to the pro-am competition. Where the amateur representation is quite heavy, some pros may be brought back for a second session of bowling. The pros who compete in the pro-am phase of all PBA tournaments receive a fixed sum of money if they are among the leading scorers.

The pros, in keeping with their image-conscious demeanor, will prove to be amiable and helpful, in addition to competent. If an amateur asks advice on any phase of his game, the pro will be quick to respond. If the amateur wants to be dead serious about the pro-am competition, or if he wants to be jovial, or a combination of both, his pro partner will strike the happy medium.

Now for the tournament proper. Here all of us are dead serious, deviating from that comportment only occasionally to break the tension out on the lanes.

If there are, say, 128 men entered in the tournament, we will be divided into two squads—A and B. Half of us will bowl the first session, let's say ten in the morning, and the other 64 will roll the second session, about one thirty in the afternoon.

All of us will bowl six games in that session and when we're done we will have completed the first round.

There will never be more than two of us assigned to any one lane. With our initial assignment to one pair of lanes, there will be four men to a pairing, and players change lanes after each game. The aim is to shoot as high as we can, because only the top scorers can keep on going in the tournament. After rolling one game on a pair of lanes (you shoot one frame on each lane and then move to the next one) you move over to another set of lanes. In this way spectators in the stands behind you can stay in place and they'll get to see almost all the bowlers, for the scene in front of them is an ever-changing one.

To simplify an already simple scoring system, the PBA uses a system called "plus and minus." It's simple and it will help you follow closely the unfolding of the sometimes dramatic proceedings in front of you.

Let's say the first game out of the box I shot a 222. The pros use a "par" system, with 200 having been arbitrarily decided upon as the par number for a professional bowler. It's a fair figure, for most of the fellows who join the PBA are at or well above that figure in their local leagues. Okay, I've just shot a 222. That means I have gone 22 pins "over par." In the upper left hand corner of my scoresheet, which is projected on the wall or screen above the bleachers, or stands, will go the number 22 and it will be printed in black by the scorekeeper. If I rolled a 194 game in my opening effort, I would have been six pins "under par" so the scorekeeper would put 6 on my scoresheet, only this time it would be printed in red ink. From then on a running account of my performance is kept right until the end of the tournament.

If I was minus 6 (6 in red) after one game, and then shot a 207 game, I'd have redeemed myself somewhat—picked up the 6 minus pins and gone one over. So, I'd now be 1 in the black. And that's the way it goes. Black is good, red isn't.

After the entire field (128 in this case) has shot the first round (or block) of six games, the second round starts, at about four thirty in the afternoon. The fellows who were on the

A squad return, shoot six more games, and then make way for the return of the B squad, who also fire six more games. At the end of that first day, all 128 bowlers will have shot twelve games—two rounds.

The following day, the order is reversed. The B squad shoots first—six games—then the A squad does the same. Now, everyone will have rolled a total of eighteen games (remember, this is the general format for PBA events, but there may be variations) and the field will be cut to the high twenty-four scorers. They'll come back to the lanes later in the day for the start of match play—man against man. Here's an explanation of how the match game phase works.

The bowlers carry over into this segment all of those pins they earned for the eighteen games that went before. Perhaps my scoresheet shows 180—and it's in the black (by the finals almost everyone will be in the black). That means that I've been shooting at an average of 210 pins per game—10 pins "over" for each of eighteen games. It may very well be that my 210 average has me way down near the end of that list of twenty-four, because a 210 average in the kind of company you keep out on the PBA tour usually isn't a fantastic showing. At any rate, it's here—in the finals—that the tournament takes a different course and we enter the match game phase— man against man competition, whereas in the qualifier we were just going for the highest score possible.

Now it's you against the other man—two of you on a pair of lanes—and you're trying to beat the other bowler as badly as you can. There's an incentive built into this portion of the tournament, which lasts twenty-four games, because in addition to earning pins through your actual score, you also get a bonus. If you beat your opponent you are credited with 30 more pins. So you can readily see why winning the game— and by as wide a margin as possible, and with as high a score as possible—is important. Let me explain that in some detail.

If I roll a 240 game and my opponent rolls a 230, I will have shot 40 pins over that par of 200 I spoke of and I will also have been given 30 pins for having won the game. Credit my "account" with a total of 70 pins. Defeat, though, has not been a total disaster for my opponent. His 230 means that he's gone 30 pins over par and he is credited with that number.

Next game, a different foe, for each man in the finals field gets to meet every other man once. After the twenty-third match game, there is a brief time out before what we call our "position round" takes place. This is the forty-second game and each man in the field is paired, for this one concluding game, with the man who is in the next place in the standings. The bowler who is the leader after forty-one games bowls the man who is in second place; bowler number three faces number four, and so on down the line. This gives each bowler in the field one last chance at maintaining his position, or improving his position possibly a place or two or more. Bowlers in the past have come from a few places down the list right into the title on the strength of a smashing final game.

If you were to shoot a perfect game—a 300—you'd again gain credit for one hundred pins on being over the 200 average, plus 30 bonus pins for registering a victory, showing how drastically and dramatically the complexion of a game can change.

The high scorer at the end of the day's bowling is the winner, but even here there can be a variation. When there is to be a television finale to a Professional Bowlers Association tournament, at the end of those forty-two games the high five scorers will return the next day. The mechanics on this day are a departure from what took place the first three days of the event.

Now it's a king-of-the-mountain setup, with the man who finished fifth facing in the opening match the man who finished fourth. The winner of that game goes on to oppose the third-place finisher, and the winner of that game next meets the number two man. The following game is the championship match, with the victor in the preceding game moving into the big one. You can see why finishing first after forty-two games is so vital. It means you automatically go into the title game, and can then wind up no worse than runner-up.

That pretty much tells you what happens in a PBA event. As a rule the competition will run four days, including one day for the pro-am. If there is to be a televised windup, five days will be required. In some tournaments, where the entry list comes close to two hundred, still another day or two may be required to trim the size of the field gradually.

It's fun and it's gratifying and if the competitive fires burn within you, as they do in most of us, bowling at the professional level is unrivaled. The money you win can be great and the feeling of fulfillment when you've won a match or taken a championship has no comparison.

Most of us spend our entire lives trying to escape the humdrum, to escape mediocrity in everything we do, in work or at play. What finer way to accomplish this than through bowling, the game that is easy for anyone to learn and improve at?

10.

A Word to the Ladies

BOWLING belongs to everyone. It puts restrictions on no one. It reaches out and beckons people who might not have realized they had any athletic ability. The young and old, weak and strong can participate and win. They can be boys or girls, men or women.

While there is a sameness in the game for everyone, everyone is an individual when it comes to bowling. Though you may have been told there is absolutely no difference between the sexes when it comes to bowling, this is not true.

Of course, the woman will take four steps and the arm swing will appear to be pretty much the same as a man's, but that's about where it ends. With rhythm playing so large a role in our sport, the women come to battle well armed. Maybe there'll be some argument from some quarters, but I'll state flatly that the girls, being the better dancers that they are, have a decided advantage when they get started in the game.

But if women have rhythm and grace and fluidity of motion going for them, men have durability and muscle on their side. To equalize somewhat the edge a man has in stamina, a woman must be certain to choose a ball of the proper weight. Bowlers of either sex aren't able to do their best if they are tired. Other than this factor, everything else is the same—timing, steps, and angle.

Years ago, all women were advised to go in for a heavier bowling ball. The thinking was that the most pins would be knocked down only by a heavier ball. But the game has changed so much that you still can come close to maximum pinfall with a ball that weighs considerably less than the allowable maximum—sixteen pounds.

I advise women—as do many other instructors—that they can use a ball that weighs anywhere from ten to fourteen pounds without fear of losing pins. Look at it this way. If you roll a sixteen-pounder and it taxes your strength or staying power, your game *must* suffer in the long run. A tired bowler never was a good one. Before I suggest a ball to a woman, I take into consideration how short or tall she is, how light or heavy, and the kind of weight she can control. The man at the pro shop should be able to tell at once what weight she can handle, just by allowing her to swing a ball. If her shoulder droops to the weight of a ball, it's too much for her.

By getting a ball of the correct weight, the woman is not compromising her game. She'll be able to sustain her accuracy, timing, and coordination and hold her own—well, almost—with the male bowler.

Some years ago I made a survey on how women bowl as compared with men. The most striking thing is that their arm swing is radically different—and that's because their arm is built differently. This accounts for the fact that many women fail to get the proper hook on the ball and as a consequence throw a backup ball—one with reverse spin. If you want to study this issue, take a look at a woman's arm from the elbow to the wrist. You'll notice that the arm goes off to the right. Their bone structure is that way.

That's why when I tutor a woman I stress that to combat this tendency to toss the reverse hook—the backup—she try to keep her wrist locked in and her thumb in the nine or ten o'clock position. The woman who wants to maintain a man-sized average should try to toss the ball conventionally, with a right to left hook. But if she finds this too difficult, then she should learn to live with the backup ball and try to become the world's best backup ball thrower.

In such case, I suggest that she take an extreme angle on the approach from the left side. That way, she'll be able to get maximum pocket power. Then, even though the woman bowler is a right-hander, she'll be getting all the advantages that a left-hander has. The reasoning here is that as long as the woman isn't capable of tossing the ball with the proper kind of hook, at least she should be able to get the ball to do more things for her. Moving to a position much like that of a left-hander is probably the necessary adjustment. It's almost the same kind of move a bowler with a conventional delivery would make if his ball was not coming into the pocket with a sharp enough angle.

The woman who is not throwing a regular hook definitely should not force herself to alter her game, unless of course, she wants to go further in bowling. While you may see countless

It's an accepted fact that a woman's forearm (*right*) is different from a man's (*left*) and that her "turned outward" arm accounts for many backup balls

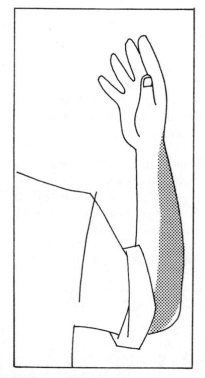 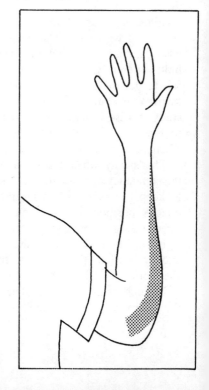

women in handicap leagues throwing a reverse hook, you'll hardly ever see any of them toss a backup when the league is on a scratch or major league level. It just won't get as many pins.

For the woman who takes her game so seriously that she wants to move on to a higher plateau, I suggest she seek instructions from a competent tutor. At the outset she'll notice a marked strain on the arm as she starts calling unused muscles into play. But quite soon, as she gets into a new groove with her release, the tenderness in her arm will vanish and bigger scores will appear. It's just a matter of drilling her in the necessity of keeping the arm and wrist locked in at the proper position.

I have changed the game of many women bowlers and it's quite gratifying to me to receive letters from many of them now and then. They've expressed their thanks to me for getting them to toss the ball "like a man." I haven't had too many letters or compliments from the ladies in the early stages, though. In the transition stage, their scores almost invariably drop—drastically in some cases. This is only normal, though. There has to be some uneasiness, some lowering of scores, in the beginning of anything new you try.

Though bowling in the accepted fashion is the way to better scoring, I will not state that all women should make an attempt to convert from backup to conventional. Some women are so frail and so leery of the changeover that the move might border on the traumatic. To these women I say stick with your best game if it makes you happy and lofty scores aren't your aim.

Except for the release point of the swing, everything else the woman bowler does—footwork, downswing and backswing—are the same. I suppose, when you come right down to it, the only way you could account for the woman not being able to roll high scores as consistently as the man is because of that built-in tendency to impart a reverse hook to the ball and the fact that most women are not as strong and do not have the stamina, the staying power.

Naturally, there has to be one exception to prove any rule. That exception would have to be a fellow named Ernie Holstery. He's a professional bowler who has competed in PBA tournaments and he throws nothing but a backup ball: mind you, a man who tosses a backup ball and competes with the world's best bowlers under tournament tension. I believe Ernie carries an average well in excess of 200. I bet that with all his talent if he were ever to go about throwing the ball the other way he'd be spectacular. But Ernie is too set in his ways by now and shoots too well to tamper with his game—the same way a woman should not if she's getting all she wants out of bowling.

A final comment on the backup ball, and the tendency of women to throw it: at best, this kind of ball is a compromise. Your shot will put you somewhere between the efficiency of a right-hander and a left-hander. You are getting no right to left movement on the ball and you are getting only an imitation of the kind of action the ball tossed by the left-hander gets. Your motion is an unnatural one and you'll have to learn to live with it and bowl with it.

Glossary

ALLEY—the area on which you bowl

ANCHOR—last man to bowl

ANGLE—relationship between your stance and the pin(s) you're shooting for

APPROACH—the area used by the bowler preparatory to tossing ball

ARCH—the width of your hook

BABY SPLIT—the 2-7 and 3-10 spares

BACKUP BALL—a ball that goes from right to left (for a right-hander)

BARMAID—a pin that is hidden by another pin

BEDPOSTS—the 7-10 split

BELLYING THE BALL—throwing the ball farther out to the right than you normally would on a lane where your ball is hooking very much

BENCH WORK—distracting conversation from the settee area

BIG EARS—the 4-6-7-10 split

BIG FILL—knocking down at least nine pins after a spare

BIG FIVE—three pins on one side, two on the other, eg., 4-7 on the left, 6-9-10 on the right

BIG FOUR—the 4-6-7-10 split

BLIND—the score given a team for an absent bowler

BLOCK—creation of a "hold area" to the pocket

BLOW—failing to pick up a spare

BLOW A RACK—a perfect strike hit

BOARD—one-inch-wide strips of wood that make up the lane

BOX—synonymous with frame

BRICKYARD—a tough house for scoring

BRIDGE—distance between finger holes on your ball

BROOKLYN—hitting the pocket (or near the pocket) on the opposite side—crossing over

BUCKET—the 2-4-5-8 spare for the right-hander, 3-5-6-9 for the left-hander

C-C—a 200 game

CHANNEL—same as gutter—dropoffs on either side of the lane

CHEESECAKE—lanes where scoring is high

CHERRY—hitting the front pin, leaving the pin or pins to the right or left still standing

CHOP—same as cherry

CHRISTMAS TREE—the 3-7-10 leave for a right-hander, 2-7-10 for a left-hander

CINCINNATI—the 8-10 split

CLEAN GAME—recording a strike or spare in every frame

COUNT—the number of pins knocked down to be added to your spare or strike

CREEPER—a slow ball

CROSS-ALLEY—playing an extreme angle from right to left or left to right

CROSSOVER—same as Brooklyn

CUSHION—padded back section behind pins

CUTOFF SHOT—failure to follow through

DEAD WOOD—pins that have been toppled

DEFLECTION—glancing action of the pins after they're struck by the ball

DEUCE—a game in the 200s

DINNER BUCKET—same as bucket

DISH—a wide ball track

DODO—an illegally weighted ball

DOUBLE—two strikes in a row

DOUBLE BALLING—throwing a second ball before the first has been returned

DOUBLE PINOCHLE—the 4-6-7-10 split

DOUBLE WOOD—one pin directly behind another

DUMMY—a score arbitrarily decided upon by a league for an absent bowler

DUTCH 200—a 200 game made by registering alternating strikes and spares

EIGHT-TEN—bowling parlance for leaving a spit on a pocket hit

ENGLISH—spin on the ball

ERROR—missing a spare

FAST—sometimes used to describe lanes on which it is difficult to throw a hook

FENCE POSTS—the 7-10 split

FILL—the number of pins knocked down after a spare

FLOATER—a ball that goes where the alley lets it

FOUL—going over the line at the end of the approach

FOUNDATION—a strike in the ninth frame

FRAME—one-tenth of a game

FUDGE SHOT—cutting down on the ball's revolutions; creating a straighter shot

FULL HIT—getting too much of the headpin

GASSING—choking up, failure to come through with the big shot or the big game at a crucial time

GOALPOSTS—the 7-10 split

GRAB—what happens when the ball suddenly starts to hook

GRASSHOPPER—A good working ball

GRAVEYARD—tough house or lanes to score in or on

GREEK CHURCH WITH A CONVENT—the 4-6-7-9-10

GROOVE—depression in the lane (track)

GUTTER—same as channel

GUTTER SHOT—sending the ball down the extreme outside of a lane

HANDICAP—adding pins to one's actual average to try and equalize competition

HIGH BOARD—a board that has risen out of position and changes the course of the ball

HIGH HIT—coming in too heavily on the headpin

HOLDING LANE—one which resists the ball's hooking action

HOLE—the pocket

JERSEY SIDE—crossing over—same as Brooklyn

JUICE—oil on the lanes

KEGLER—synonymous with bowler

KICKBACK—side boards at pit end of the lane off which pins carom

KINDLING WOOD—light pins

KINGPIN—the 5 pin

KITTY—money collected either as "penalty" for missing certain shots, or side wagers among team members

LAZY TEN—a 10 pin that teeters before it totters

LEAVE—pins standing after the first shot

LIFT—a right to left spin with an upward pull of fingers

LIGHT HIT—not getting enough of the pocket

LOFTING—throwing the ball too far out on the lane

LOOPER—a ball that goes far to the right before coming back (same as bellying)

LOW HIT—a ball that comes in lightly on the headpin

MAPLES—the pins (even though they're covered with plastic)

MARK—a strike or spare

MISS—an error (not getting a spare)

MIXER—a good working ball

MOTHER-IN-LAW—the 7 pin

MOVE IN—starting from near a center position on the approach

MOVE OUT—starting from a corner position on the approach

MULE EARS—the 7-10 split

MURPHY—the baby split

NOSE DIVE—strike on a dead-center hit

OPEN FRAME—failing to get a mark

OUT AND IN—same as bellying the ball

OUTSIDE LINE—playing certain lanes from a corner position

PACKING—same as count or fill

PART OF THE BUILDING—derisive statement by bowler to explain why the 7 or 10 pin failed to fall

PICKET FENCE—the 1-2-4-7 or 1-3-6-10

PINBOY—boy who set up pins before introduction of automatic machines

PINCHING THE BALL—squeezing too hard

PIT—space behind the pin deck into which the pins fall

PITCH—angle at which the finger holes in a ball are drilled

POCKET—the strike zone

POISON IVY—the 3-6-10

PUDDLE—a gutter ball

PUNCHING OUT—striking out in the last frame

RAIL—same as split in some sections

RAKE—the sweeper bar on the automatic machines that pushes dead wood into the pit

RUNNING LANE—a lane that takes a hook; opposite of holding

RUNWAY—the approach in some places

SANDWICH GAME—same as Dutch 200

SCRATCH—using an actual score without any handicap

SHOTGUN SHOT—a ball thrown from the hip

SLEEPER—a hidden pin

SLOTS—alleys that are easy to score on

SPAN—distance between the thumb and finger holes

SPLASH—a strike where the pins seem to "explode" off the deck

SPOT—a place on the lane at which a bowler aims

STEAL—to get more pins on a shot than you thought you deserved

STIFF LANE—one that resists a hook

STRAPPING THE BALL—getting all the fingers and lift into the ball that you can

STRIKING OUT—getting three strikes in the tenth frame

SWEEPER—a ball that seems to sweep the pins off the deck

SWING OUT—letting your arm swing away from your body on the release

SWISHER—getting a strike by blowing the 5 pin to the left (reverse for a left-hander)

TANDEM—pins that stand one behind the other. Such as the 1-5, 2-8, and 3-9

TAP—when one pin is left standing after an apparently perfect strike ball

TELEPHONE POLES—the 7-10 and in some places heavy pins

THIN—a light hit in the pocket

THROWING ROCKS—tossing many strike balls

TILT 10—what happens when the 6 pin nicks the 10 and makes it fall

TRIP 4—where the 2 pin ricochets off the side board and knocks over the 4

TURKEY—three strikes in a row

WALL SHOT—getting a strike by means of pins ricocheting off sideboards

WASHOUT—the 1-2-10 or 1-2-4-10 spare. For a left-hander, the 1-3-7 or 1-3-6-7

WOODEN BOTTLES—pins

WOOLWORTH—the 5-10 split

WORKING BALL—one that has good speed and hooking action when it reaches the pins